I'm Sorry I Broke Your Company

▼

When Management Consultants Are the Problem, Not the Solution

Karen Phelan

BK

Berrett–Koehler Publishers, Inc.
San Francisco
a BK Business book

Berrett-Koehler Publishers, Inc.
235 Montgomery Street, Suite 650
San Francisco, CA 94104-2916
Tel: (415) 288-0260 Fax: (415) 362-2512 www.bkconnection.com

Ordering Information
Quantity sales. Special discounts are available on quantity purchases by corporations, associations, and others. For details, contact the "Special Sales Department" at the Berrett-Koehler address above.
Individual sales. Berrett-Koehler publications are available through most bookstores. They can also be ordered directly from Berrett-Koehler: Tel: (800) 929-2929; Fax: (802) 864-7626; www.bkconnection.com
Orders for college textbook/course adoption use. Please contact Berrett-Koehler: Tel: (800) 929-2929; Fax: (802) 864-7626.
Orders by U.S. trade bookstores and wholesalers. Please contact Ingram Publisher Services: Tel: (800) 509-4887; Fax: (800) 838-1149; E-mail: customer.service@ingram publisherservices.com; or visit www.ingrampublisherservices.com/Ordering for details about electronic ordering.

Berrett-Koehler and the BK logo are registered trademarks of Berrett-Koehler Publishers, Inc.

Printed in the United States of America

Berrett-Koehler books are printed on long-lasting acid-free paper. When it is available, we choose paper that has been manufactured by environmentally responsible processes. These may include using trees grown in sustainable forests, incorporating recycled paper, minimizing chlorine in bleaching, or recycling the energy produced at the paper mill.

Library of Congress Cataloging-in-Publication Data
Phelan, Karen.
  I'm sorry I broke your company : when management consultants are the problem, not the solution / Karen Phelan.—1st ed.
   p. cm.
  Includes bibliographical references and index.
   ISBN 978-1-60994-739-2 (pbk.)
1. Management. 2. Management consultants. 3. Reengineering (Management)
4. Organizational effectiveness. 5. Personnel management. I. Title.
HD31.P432 2013
658.4'6—dc23   2012034724

FIRST EDITION
18 17 16 15 14 13   10 9 8 7 6 5 4 3 2 1

Cover/jacket designer: Irene Morris
Cover art: © Steve Hix/Corbis
Interior design and type: Beverly Butterfield, Girl of the West Productions
Editor: PeopleSpeak

I'm Sorry I
Broke Your
Company

Contents

Preface

∇

I'm sorry. I really am. Does it help if I say I meant well? To be honest, though, it's not entirely my fault. We're all victims of a flawed business model. What happens when you hire new employees fresh out of prestigious business schools? What are they good at? Performing logical analyses, learning models and theories and applying them, and creating new models and theories. What are they most lacking? Real-world experience. So how were we to know that the models and theories were wrong? They were elegant and logical, and based on our experience with models and theories, that's the mark of excellence. Fortunately, I was a little bit different from the rest. My degrees were in engineering and science, and I had a brief foray into a scientific career in a military laboratory before becoming a consultant. I knew a little about real-world results not matching the theories. But I must say, I was as gullible as the next consultant—at first.

Unfortunately, few statistically sound, well-managed studies prove the accuracy of management theories. Management theories rarely get peer-reviewed or validated by a third party before they become part of the accepted body of knowledge. Most of the evidence is anecdotal, and many of the existing studies have a degree of self-interest. (How many companies will admit that their multimillion-dollar restructuring effort had few benefits?) So I am going to tell you about my personal journey of enlightenment, where during a thirty-plus-year career as a management consultant and manager in Fortune 100s, I slowly and steadily realized that many of our management theories are wrong.

On behalf of all the management consultants who've been working in your companies over the last three decades, proselytizing about management by objectives and competitive strategy, I apologize. I'm sorry I broke your company.

Introduction

Most people, if not all, have a hidden talent—some goofy or useful ability that they share with few other humans. I once met a woman with an uncanny ability to call coin tosses. I know another woman who can mimic the tones of a telephone and get her voice mail without pressing buttons. My older son can manipulate three-dimensional images of objects in his mind. When we built models together, I noticed that he built his in his head first. My younger son converses in his sleep. I don't mean he utters random words or phrases. You can have an entire conversation with him while he is sleeping. My husband can dead reckon anywhere through the woods. If you ever need to get out of the woods quickly, he can navigate a path without a GPS and get you within one hundred feet of your car. I have a skill, too. I realized exactly what it was only a few years ago.

In 2006 I attended a Sloan School class on systems dynamics. Our first task was to break into teams and play the beer distribution game, a simulation of the supply chain of a beer manufacturer. The game illustrated the bullwhip effect, a phenomenon well-known to people who work in supply chains. The effect shows that small variations at one end of the chain can become amplified along the chain, resulting in large variations at the other end. A few minutes into the game, I realized what was going on and figured out the correct order quantities while the rest of the class struggled. I am familiar with supply-chain problems, so I thought little of it. However, in problem after problem, the answer was just plainly obvious to me. While everyone else was documenting cause-and-effect loops, I thought about the problems and found the answers. My classmates marveled at my ability, and I became something of a phenomenon. Only I felt like a fraud. Yes, I could solve all the systems problems in my head in a few minutes, but I didn't have a remarkable computer-like ability to solve systems problems. My talent is empathy—being able to put myself in someone else's shoes.

With each problem, I immersed myself in the situation and pretended I was there, making decisions as the various actors until I found the one that worked. How I really differed from everyone else in the class, including the instructor, was that I knew these problems weren't about supply chains, factory maintenance, improvement initiatives, or construction schedules. They were about people reacting to circumstances. Every business problem is about people reacting to circumstances.

Textbooks, consultants, and experts blame the bullwhip effect on forecast errors, unpredictable demand, poor information, poor inventory management, and so on. What they don't mention is that the bullwhip effect is primarily caused by emotions. It is caused by fear when demand falls off slightly, and people become scared and order less and less all along the chain. It is caused by optimism when demand increases slightly, and people hope demand grows and worry that they won't have enough supply so they order too much. It is caused by mistrust as each person adds to or subtracts from his order to cover his ass if the supplier can't ship as planned or the customer changes her mind. The only way to eliminate the bullwhip effect is to eliminate the fear, hope, and mistrust of the people ordering inventory.

I wrote this book because, after a thirty-year-long career, I am tired of pretending. I've had to do a lot of pretending—pretending that the inventory management system I am implementing is the answer when I am really getting each part of the supply chain to trust each other, pretending to reengineer the new product development process when I am really getting the Sales, Marketing, and Research and Development (R&D) Departments to work together better, pretending that my amazing ability to solve problems is due to computer-like thinking rather than human-like imagining. Most of all, I am tired of seeing employees treated as assets that need to be monitored, measured, standardized, and optimized. I can't be honest about what I do because no one would buy my services if I said that I help people work together better. Instead, I pretend to sell methodologies, models, metrics, processes, and systems.

As a young consultant, I created many models, processes, and programs, all with the purpose of taking the variability out of tasks, the emotions out of decisions, and the judgment out of management. In short, I was trying to eliminate the human element from running a business. I was not alone. Over the last two decades, management methods have proliferated and embedded themselves as corporate best practices with the goals of improving efficiencies, standardizing skills, and optimizing performance. Balanced scorecards, pay for performance, core competence development, process reengineering, leadership assessments, management models, competitive strategy, and cascading performance measures are some of the models that are now entrenched in business management, even though there is little evidence that they work as advertised. All these models and theories attempt to dehumanize the workplace, and they have succeeded, though not as intended. People are treated like machines that have to be maximized until they break, and all their unique and goofy talents never see the light of day.

We have been led to believe by management gurus and management consultancies that businesses are logical and run by the numbers and that their models and theories will provide step-by-step instructions on how to succeed. Companies try to implement these models or make decisions strictly by the numbers and never realize the expected successes because businesses are not actually rational. Human assets are not a part of a business. If you take away the human assets, you don't have a business, just a bunch of offices and equipment that can't do anything. Businesses are people—irrational, emotional, unpredictable, creative, oddly gifted, and sometimes ingenious people who don't operate according to the theories. This book is a reminder that we need to stop trying to dehumanize the workplace and that if you manage the people element, you pretty much have everything covered. This book is intended for consultants, people who hire consultants, non-consultants, and anyone who is tired of pretending that modern management practices work. If you have ever been at work and wondered if everyone else was insane, you are not alone. I wrote this book for you.

▷ Why I blame management consultants

The term "consultant" is used very loosely. Anyone who is a contractor to a business is considered a consultant. Plus, there are all sorts of technology consultants, marketing consultants, and design consultants. When I use the term "management consultant," I am talking about those who work with the top layers of corporate management and advise them on what to do. More specifically, my ire is mostly addressed at the large consultancies that hire MBAs straight out of school and arm them with spreadsheets, pro forma methodologies, incoherent jargon, and a not-small amount of arrogance. I blame these people for conceiving and propagating the many management myths that are the roots of some of the biggest problems in business today—lack of innovation, short-term focus, obsession with financial gains over creating valuable products and services, and stressed-out, overworked, and disengaged employees.

Rather than focusing on the obvious question—How can my business make life better?—corporate leaders have spent the last few decades fixating on other, less-meaningful questions like,

- How do I gain a competitive advantage?
- How do I maximize my shareholder value?
- How do I increase my bottom line (both personal and corporate)?
- How do I optimize the efficiency of my human assets?

The result is lean and mean companies that operate alike, offer copycat products and services, and are dependent on acquisitions for growth. Many of these problems are rooted in the accepted management wisdom that abounds with little proof of veracity. The beginnings of all this management dogma started with one or more management consultants. The best analogy I can use to explain this cycle is diet and exercise fads. It seems like every year brings a doctor or fitness expert who has found the solution for weight loss. That solution may be a miracle food or a rigorous diet program or a new exercise regimen. However, none of these fads work, and worse, they often result in yo-yo dieting that leads to more weight gain and overall poor health. To be healthy, you need to eat a variety of foods in moderation and get plenty of exercise and enough sleep. The secret to weight loss is the same secret that everyone has known forever. There is no secret.

Similarly, every year, management consultants develop some new model or theory that will be the answer to all your business problems. Visit the website of any consultancy and you will see that it sells "business solutions." Management consultants strive to achieve thought leadership by creating new models and theories that hopefully will be adopted widely by businesses and make them famous (and rich). However, all this has just led us to fad after fad after fad. The widespread adoption of each fad brings with it its own set of problems that lays the groundwork for the next fad. Competitive strategy based on external factors led to competence strategy based on internal capabilities, which led to blue ocean strategy based on top-down ideation, which led to adaptive strategy based on bottom-up responses to the marketplace. Each one corrects the deficiencies of the former fad but then creates deficiencies of its own. The result is a vicious cycle similar to dieting, gaining weight, more dieting, and more weight gain. The only way to stop the fads is to stop the management consultants creating and selling them.

▷ About this book

This is not an academic book offering original research or proof positive of my ideas. This is the story of how I came to realize that everything I believed about business was wrong. It's my story woven with the rise and fall of some of the management fads I helped propagate. I chose the examples based on how they changed my thinking about what I was doing. The first three chapters recount my experiences with strategy development, process improvements, and metrics implementations. Many of the examples in these chapters are from my early career as a young consultant, when I worked for large consultancies. The next four chapters discuss the methods that fall under the banner of "talent management" and cover performance management systems, management models, high-potential programs, and leadership competencies. Most of the examples in these chapters relate to my experiences in a later part of my career in the corporate world, where I got to live through many of the methods I had helped implement.

I would like to be very clear about my purpose. The point of this book is to debunk the conventional business wisdom and not to add to it. Although I offer my recommendations, I offer them as alternatives to the theories that don't work. For the most part, I recommend replacing the model or process with a candid conversation among colleagues. Unfortunately, I haven't done a major study to show that improving dialogue and relationships has a business benefit. I will let you be the judge of that theory. Fortunately, debunking a theory is much easier. It requires only one piece of evidence that disproves it. I'm going to repeat this because most consultants I know have a hard time understanding this: you need only one piece of contrary evidence to disprove a theory. Proving a theory to be true is much harder, requiring that it works in all situations. This is where management consultants often get it wrong. They find something that works once or twice and label it a best practice to be followed by everyone when it is useful only in a specific situation.

I offer recommendations and alternatives as a starting point to help us get out of the faulty thinking that pervades today, like "You can't manage what you can't measure." (Well, yes you can!) I am in no way suggesting that I have the solutions. I'm just suggesting that instead of implementing a method that is often wrong, we try doing something else that might work. I'm suggesting that we cut through the dogma to find the kernel of truth and base our new solutions on that truth. Isn't it better to have only a chance of being wrong than to most certainly be wrong? I think that's pretty obvious. In fact, if I were to describe what this book is about, I think it's about the really obvious.

1

Strategic Planning Can't Predict the Future

Strategy Development Is a Vision Quest

▷ **The downside of having a strategy is missed opportunities**

In 1980, Michael Porter, a Harvard professor and founder of the Monitor Group consulting company, published a book called *Competitive Strategy: Techniques for Analyzing Industries and Competitors* and helped usher in the modern age of business strategy consultants that exploded in the '80s and '90s. While boutique consultancies, namely Bain and the Boston Consulting Group, were formed in the '60s, either their client base was limited or their models dealt with managing cash. Actually formulating a business strategy was something of a black art consisting of one part analysis, one part experience, and a whole lot of magic—kind of like a corporate version of the Native American drug-induced rite of self-discovery, the vision quest. However, businesses tend to prefer analysis, structure, and tangibility over magic, art, and lucid dreaming. Michael Porter's book not only codified how to create a strategy, with step-by-step instructions on how to do the analysis, it also codified what the strategies should be.

Besides embedding the phrase "competitive advantage" into the corporate psyche, Porter introduced two well-known models in his book. The first was the five-forces model, which showed the external and internal factors facing businesses: competitors, potential entrants, potential substitutes, buyers, and suppliers. This was the framework for performing the industry analysis and was introduced in chapter 1. The second chapter offered up Porter's second most famous item: the three generic business strategies of lost-cost producer, differentiation, and focused offering. Depending on your position in the industry, you would choose one of the three strategies to gain a competitive advantage. The rest of the book is an incredibly comprehensive blueprint for analyzing competitors, anticipating their potential responses, and dissecting industry structures to determine alternative strategies—all with a multitude of checklists to use. After several attempts at reading this book and eventually struggling through it, I came to realize that perhaps the reason why the five-forces model and the generic strategies were the only models to become part of the management lexicon was that few people were able to read beyond the first two chapters. With Porter's models and checklists, consultants had both a method and a set of answers that could be packaged and implemented by any reasonably smart college graduate. The art part of strategy formulation was replaced by a series of checklists and a multiple-choice option and made available to anyone.

When I was a consultant at Deloitte Haskins & Sells (DH&S) in the late '80s, Porter's book was required reading. DH&S was undergoing a major shift in its management consulting arm. When I joined, each office had its own local consulting practice and sold whatever work it was able to, usually small jobs to small local clients. After I had been in the New Jersey office about a year, the consulting leadership decided to develop a national consulting practice that would bring us more prestige, Fortune 500 clients, and bigger engagements with more revenues. It started with a strategic vision of organizing around industrial expertise, like banking and manufacturing, and developing service offerings. Local offices would be part of a national practice depending on the industries at their locations. New Jersey was a hotbed of pharmaceutical manufacturing, so we were part of the manufacturing practice. Because of our proximity to New York City, we also had a designated financial services practice. In addition to serving our local markets, we would also share resources nationally. This would provide a depth of experience often missing locally. At the time, this seemed like a good idea to me. Designated service offerings versus ad hoc services, national practice versus local, Fortune 500 clients versus smaller businesses—it seemed like a no-brainer. Who wouldn't want to be part of a strategic vision?

Part of this national practice vision required those of us in New Jersey to target some of the well-known pharmaceutical manufacturers. None of us had any pharmaceutical experience, so I, the most junior member, was tasked with doing a pharmaceutical industry analysis so that we could better position services to this very profitable industry. Using Porter's book, I had the step-by-step instruction guide for doing an industry analysis. What I remember most about doing this was how difficult it was to obtain the necessary information. This was before the Internet, and digging up information required both calling companies posing as a shareholder and making numerous trips to the library to sift through syndicated databases. Given my difficulties, I wondered how thorough and comprehensive any competitor analysis could really be. You would really have to work at a given company to get all its information. Despite having gaps in information, I managed to put together what looked like a comprehensive analysis of the industry with lots of graphs and charts and a summary of strengths, weaknesses, opportunities, and threats. I learned a great deal from this process and developed an in-depth knowledge of the pharmaceutical industry that I would use later in my career.

I wish I could say that my foray into developing a strategic analysis of the pharmaceutical industry was the beginning of a successful pharmaceutical practice, but shortly afterward, DH&S made the decision to merge with Touche Ross, and Touche took over the consulting practice, dissolving ours. Our strategy of becoming strategy consultants was foiled by external influences! If we had been any good, we would have seen that coming. At the time, I was astonished at this turn of events. Touche Ross was still using the local office, ad hoc model. We had a *strategy*! We had centers of expertise! Yet Touche Ross had more work. While we had been focusing internally to pursue bigger clients, our actual sales had been dropping. Touche Ross was still bringing in a steady stream of client engagements using the old model. As a result, most of the DH&S consultants were let go because we had no ongoing client accounts or important relationships to bring to the merged practice. While we had developed some expertise, some service offerings, and an organization structure, we hadn't developed the client base to go with them. In hindsight, I was spending a lot of time in the office doing analyses and not much time on billable client work.

Touche Ross had a much broader practice. It had numerous services I had never heard of in nonprofits, hospitals, and Medicare, Medicaid, and other government organizations, like conducting patient surveys and ferreting out fraudulent claims. While Deloitte was consolidating around financial services and manufacturing service offerings, Touche was just seizing whatever opportunities presented themselves.

To be fair, all the accounting firms did eventually develop more organized practices with service offerings, but these practices eventually emerged from the work they were doing. DH&S tried to use a top-down model dictated by a handful of managing partners based on their own experiences. Although it sounded good in theory, we missed a lot of opportunities, especially with the assumption that manufacturing would continue to be the bulk of the US economy. I learned that pursuing a strategy can actually have a downside, that of lost opportunities. Rather than responding to the marketplace by taking whatever client work presented itself, we tried to dictate the marketplace. With our single-minded focus, we ignored new markets and new services and focused on a vision we couldn't bring to fruition. I wish I could say that this was an isolated experience, but I would live through something similar two more times, with Gemini Consulting and Pfizer.

▷ Managing by the numbers only manages the numbers

In 1990, I joined the United Research Company, an operations and organization improvement consulting group, while it was undergoing a merger with the MAC Group, a strategy house, to become Gemini Consulting. For a few short years, Gemini became the go-to consultants to drastically reduce the number of permanent employees and increase efficiencies under the banner "business process reengineering." Unlike other consulting companies of that time, we actually implemented the recommended changes and promised specific results in the form of cost savings. Every consulting engagement had a benefits case that detailed the savings we promised to deliver. During the economic downturn of this period, Gemini became very successful at helping companies downsize, and we grew rapidly. Our engagements also became larger and larger, and in some cases we "transformed" entire divisions and even entire companies at one time.

Another entity famous for downsizing was General Electric. Under CEO Jack Welch, GE grew to become the largest company in the world through approximately one thousand acquisitions. However, he divested and laid off as much as he acquired, firing over one hundred thousand workers, almost 25 percent of the company, leaving empty buildings in his wake and earning him the name Neutron Jack. His philosophy was that a business should be number one or two in its industry in terms of market share or else be sold off. This was not an isolated or radical viewpoint. The Boston Consulting Group, one of the oldest and most prestigious strategy consulting companies, had long advocated for investing in business units that have a high market share and growth potential (stars) and divesting the "dogs" that don't. Because of GE's success, Welch's philosophy and methods were widely copied by other companies and deemed best practices.

One of his other much-admired and imitated philosophies was the concept of creating shareholder value, whereby a company ensures that shareholders get a better return from its stock than they could from other investments. A mathematical formula shows that shareholder value is a function of a company's return on its assets (ROA) and its investments (ROI). Together this is the return on equity, or ROE. This philosophy created a fixation on a bunch of financial measures—for example, ROE, ROA, ROI, and ROCE (return on capital employed). Managing these metrics would result in positive cash flows that would be reflected in the stock price, thus earning the shareholders better returns. (Of course, this is predicated on the efficient market hypothesis, which assumes rational entities buy stocks based on these types of calculations. This all falls apart if people purchase the stock because the logo looks pretty.) Hence, in addition to the traditional measures of revenues and profits, executives in the late '80s and early '90s became fixated on market share, share price, and a variety of financial metrics to determine how productive the company's assets and investments were. Management by the numbers and a focus on asset efficiency were in full swing.

I got my first taste of this mathematical approach to management on a very large business transformation project. Gemini was working at an underperforming business unit of a huge chemical manufacturer and tasked with improving its return on equity (ROE). An initial team of consultants had identified ROE as the weak point in the company's shareholder value drivers, so our main focus was to increase the "productivity of its assets," that is, cut costs, and to improve the returns on its investments. One of the first things we did was set up a huge war room where we hung charts and graphs showing our progress against our savings goals. One of the most impressive charts was a three-foot-wide bar chart labeled "Asset Productivity," which showed revenues generated per square foot for every facility. Of course, the least productive assets were the sprawling corporate headquarters and a massive research center. Realistically, we couldn't sell those off, but the chart did teach me an important lesson about consulting. Dividing one measure by another and then plotting the results on a fancy graph impresses clients. That and charting one measure along an x-axis and another along a y-axis, resulting in a quadrant chart, are probably two of the most important consulting skills you can have.

I led a team focused on improving the return on capital expenditures. In the company's current state, the business unit leaders had the decision-making authority to invest in capital as they saw fit. As part of our consulting intervention, my team put a standard portfolio review process in place where every business would use the same decision criteria and financial analyses to judge capital projects. The goal was to pool capital expenditures across all the business units and then to choose projects with the highest ROI. We developed a decision model that assigned a score based on the strategic value to the company and the financials of the proposed investment, and we implemented a new process for managing capital projects with a series of cross-business-unit meetings to act as gates for selecting the portfolio.

As a dry run, several of the current projects were put through the process. One project stood out like a sore thumb. The newest business unit had a very profitable product line and had been rapidly expanding its capacity. It had another capital project on the slate. Several executives at headquarters feared that this project would create an overcapacity situation and the profit margins would decrease. Given the rate of expansion in the past, it didn't make sense to build yet another plant. The accepted wisdom on the leadership team was that the business unit head was intent on building an empire at the expense of profits. Using the new capital projects decision model, we calculated the risks involved and the impact on margins and concluded that the plant would not meet the threshold ROI. Of course, the projected revenues were a best guess, but we based our projections on a straight-line increase in the current demand.

The head of this business unit was angry with our result. I considered this conflict to be a test of whether my client could exercise the discipline needed to judge the business units objectively or whether politics would win out, as it often does. I was disappointed to learn several months later that this project had gotten the go-ahead, and I assumed it was because of politics. Years later, though, I learned that my incremental projections for future demand were grossly inadequate. This particular field underwent an immense wave of innovation that spurred all sorts of new applications and end products that couldn't have been imagined at the time. The actual growth in demand was way off my charts. The company would need lots of additional capacity.

Another team on this project was devoted to developing a new strategy for generating revenue growth and improving market share. They were called the "Strategic Intent/Core Competence" team, based on a new trend in strategy from the Harvard Business School and elaborated on in a book called *Competing for the Future*, by Gary Hamel and C. K. Prahalad. The key point of the book was that companies needed to anticipate and shape the future of the industry by building core competencies, a collection of skills unique to that company. For example, Canon used its competencies in precision mechanics, fine optics, microelectronics, and electronic imaging to expand its product line from cameras into market leadership in copiers, fax machines, and printers. In many ways, the book was a much-needed antithesis to Michael Porter and the warfare paradigm, where everyone fights over a limited market share. *Competing for the Future* was about creating new market opportunities and developing unique capabilities, not determining a position based on what your competitors were doing. By building core competencies, companies would have capabilities that their competitors couldn't replicate easily and would be in a position to control the future and not just react to it. To contrast, Porter's work said that the market forces and industry determined what kind of strategic course should be pursued, while Hamel and Prahalad said that internal capabilities should not only determine the strategy but shape the industry. The latter is a very appealing idea because it essentially means you can control your future.

The first step of the SICC team was to determine the client's unique core competencies. Unfortunately, the only area where the client significantly outperformed its competitors was in performing financial analyses. That couldn't be leveraged to create a strategy for a manufacturing company. Without finding unique capabilities to leverage into an overarching strategy that would shape the future, the team fell back upon Porter's methods and embarked on a "differentiation strategy." The differentiation would be to create a premium product and with it a whole new brand and a new sales channel.

To make a long story short, we consultants walked away from that project contented and excited about having transformed an underperforming business by developing a premium brand, taking out a lot of costs by eliminating assets (including humans), and putting more meaningful decision making into its capital expenditures. However, in reality, the business continued to underperform, and ten years later it was spun off and sold with the exception of the business unit that had been expanding its capacity. I don't know if it was sheer luck or business acumen, but that business-unit head had an insight into his business no one else possessed, and he made the right decision to add capacity, even though the projected numbers didn't support it. Who could have predicted that so many new end products would be invented? To be honest, we did a terrible job of trying to shape the future. Heck, we couldn't even predict it accurately.

▷ Predicting the future is risky business

The problem with these strategic plans is that they require you to predict the future. I have to admit I experienced a perverse sense of enjoyment reading the case examples in my old strategy books. *Competing for the Future* uses NEC, Motorola, JVC, and EDS as examples of best practices, and what especially amused me was the story of the VCR and how JVC beat Sony to market dominance. Lots of the examples are of Japanese companies because at the time, Japanese companies and the Japanese economy were booming and outperforming American companies in many industries. What struck me about rereading Porter's book is the emphasis on manufacturing. Although he mentions other industries, most of the examples are about manufacturers, and he frequently mentions building capacity as a strategic maneuver and plants and equipment as barriers to entry and exit. Today, our biggest industries are health care, retail, financial services, and manufacturing, with manufacturing on the decline. Plus, I giggled every time he mentioned "mini-computers." This isn't a criticism of Hamel, Prahalad, and Porter. They are brilliant thinkers. It just highlights how difficult it is to predict the future.

If these brilliant, Harvard-educated guys can't predict the future very well, how can the rest of us expect to do so?

If you pick up any decade-old business book that uses company examples to illustrate its points, at least half of those companies will no longer be performing well. GE was used as a benchmark for companies in the 1990s, and lots of its practices were imitated. Today, few would copy a GE practice. Even Jack Welch himself has backpedaled on the importance of shareholder value. If you are looking for a company to emulate, Google and Apple are the likely choices.

The problem with executing strategic plans is that they are predicated on your ability to predict economic conditions, industry changes, competitor actions, and customer desires. However, no one can do this with any kind of reliability. This is why financial experts recommend investing in index funds. The majority of mutual fund managers cannot outperform the indexes they are trying to beat, and they have tons of research and researchers at their disposal. They come from all the best schools. Yet they cannot predict the future performance of stocks with any reliability or accuracy. Of all the world-class economists whose jobs are to predict the future, almost no one saw the financial crisis of 2008 coming. Yet it is a business best practice to try to predict the future and enact a plan around that future vision. This is what companies are supposed to do to succeed.

After Gemini had become successful at process reengineering, its leadership team decided that Gemini needed a strategy to take us to the next level. A small team of leaders decided that our future was "business transformation," and Gemini would own this term and offer all its services under this brand. This approach would tackle business strategy, business processes, information technology (IT), and organizational design in one fell swoop, completely remaking a company. Although that sounds altruistic, it was really consultant-speak for extra big cost-cutting projects. Except for desperate companies, who else would want a complete makeover? The business transformation strategy was communicated to all employees, and managers were told to sell work that fit the transformation tenets. Although we had some huge transformation engagements at the time, our bread and butter—as is the case generally for consultants—was a steady stream of small projects. We were no longer going to pursue these.

Unfortunately for us, but fortunately for the rest of the world, the economy picked up, companies were no longer desperate to downsize. No one was interested in buying business transformation because it is essentially a disruptive, costly, and painful process. Although our leadership eventually realized this folly, we had become a company associated with massive downsizing. Whenever "Gemini" was mentioned in a competitive bid, the client's employees trembled. Companies were tired of downsizing. This new thing called the Internet and its associate, e-commerce, about which we knew nothing, were all the rage. Gemini started cutting its own heads, something it knew how to do well. All our best consultants started to leave for competitors, and Gemini dissipated within a few short years. It is now a small organizational development group within Cap Gemini Ernst & Young and has a few small offices outside the United States. This outcome was particularly ironic as transforming companies through strategy development and process reengineering was our business, and we had the best tools and smartest people at our disposal.

A few years later, after I had left the chaos of the consulting world for a more stable corporate job, I lived through a similar experience with Pfizer. Under Hank McKinnell, Pfizer's strategy was to use its massive sales force (almost twice as large as the nearest competitor's) to create blockbuster drugs. In the early 2000s, Pfizer had an impressive array of multibillion-dollar drugs and more in the pipeline. It had turned Lipitor into the best-selling drug in history, had created a whole new market with Viagra, and was buying Pharmacia to exploit Celebrex in the same way. At the time, Pfizer wouldn't even consider developing a drug that didn't have a potential market value of $1 billion. Also in this time frame, Pfizer began to shed its nonpharmaceutical businesses because it wanted to focus on its core business of proprietary pharmaceuticals, and these side businesses were diluting its earnings per share. Pharmaceutical companies have traditionally diversified to mitigate the risks of drug development. Pharmaceuticals may have high profit margins, but the chances of developing a useful and popular drug, never mind a blockbuster, are pretty slim. Needless to say, over the next few years, Pfizer's pipeline of potential blockbusters, Celebrex, Bextra, torcetrapib, Exubera, Chantix, and Rezulin, went bust. The Pfizer stock price declined from forty-two dollars to seventeen dollars during this time (before the market crash of 2008), and the company chewed through both Hank McKinnell and his handpicked successor, Jeff Kindler, in five years.

I have worked for only four companies in my career, and this is what happened to three of them. (I left the fourth after a poorly managed acquisition—so poor that the corporate leadership needed to testify before Congress.) These anecdotes about strategies going awry are not the exception. This is how strategy is done. If you look at them from a textbook perspective, Gemini and Pfizer did many things right. From the core competence perspective, they both built upon their own unique capabilities. At Gemini, it was process reengineering and results delivery capabilities. At Pfizer, it was its sales juggernaut. They also anticipated the future and conceived an innovative strategy that would shape the marketplace. From a Porter perspective, they pursued a differentiation strategy that would result in a significant

competitive advantage. Gemini would own the business transformation consulting market, and Pfizer would turn drugs into
blockbuster drugs. Best yet, aligning with the Jack Welch and
Boston Consulting Group tenets, these strategies would lead to
unbridled growth and market leadership. Plus, they were based
on past successes in the marketplace. The strategies themselves
passed these textbook tests, and even better, the companies also
executed the strategies well.

If you look at these strategies from a layperson's perspective,
rather than a strategy analyst's, you're likely to say, "What were
they thinking?" In the consulting world, the Holy Grail is big
projects at Fortune 500 clients. This is the consulting equiva-
lent of premium products with repeat buyers—a highly profitable
business model with low conversion costs. This is the strategy
both DH&S and Gemini were pursuing and the place where
most consulting firms want to be. The problem with targeting
Fortune 500 clients is that there aren't thousands of them. There
are only 500. And there are only so many big projects a company
of any size wants to take on. Getting a big project at a big client is
a little like winning the lottery. In comparison, Pfizer's strategy of
developing only blockbuster drugs is a lot like the strategy of trying to win the lottery by buying only winning tickets. Of course,
every pharma company wants blockbuster drugs. It's just that drug
development is a very risky business, and most of the promising
molecules won't result in any drug at all.

What would lead smart companies like Pfizer and Gemini
to create untenable strategies? Let's review the typical process for
strategy development. First, it is a given that corporate success is
predicated on a leader developing a corporate vision of the future,
which by definition is predicting the future. The way to develop
the future vision is to hire consultants who do lots of research on
the industry and trends and write all this up in a report. Next, the

consultants bring a small group of the leadership team together to brainstorm an overall vision and strategic goals based on their findings. In the strategy world, "big, hairy, audacious goals" (per Jim Collins), like "being number one or two," "new market creation," and "continuous double digit growth," are encouraged. If you are going to dream, you might as well dream big! Once that vision is created, the leader needs to persuade the rest of the organization to believe the vision, and then management ensures that the organization takes only those actions that would lead to the creation of that vision. Businesses need to focus their resources and therefore can't expend resources on anything other than achieving the strategy.

To summarize, the current state of strategy development and execution is this:

1. Predict the future.
2. Define an audacious stretch goal based on that prediction.
3. Persuade other, more pragmatic people, who weren't involved in creating the goal and who typically need their monthly salaries, to work toward it.
4. Work on nothing else.
5. Celebrate success!

Are you laughing or are you crying? I mean, it is pretty funny except for being so sad. Companies go bankrupt and people lose their jobs because of this thinking. Even funnier is that neither Porter, Prahalad, Hamel, Welch, nor BCG or any of the other strategy houses devised this process. It is the collective sum of the thinking around strategy, and in this case, the sum is much, much less than the parts. Obviously, this is not the right way to plan the future of a company.

▷ Planning for the future and predicting the future are not the same thing

Let's go back to the beginning, before Porter and everyone else. The basis for corporate strategy development was warfare; that's where the term "strategy" came from. Porter's book is full of warfare terminology such as "competitive warfare," "defensive moves," "retaliation," and "fighting brand" and assumes that a company needs to beat its competition to win. Although I don't agree that corporations need to engage in battle to succeed, I do want to understand how warfare theory can contribute to business strategy.

Back in the '80s, some of the other popular books on strategy were treatises on war, like Sun Tzu's *Art of War*. I don't particularly care for this book because it's a listing of aphorisms, and it's over two thousand years old. The book I chose to teach me about battle strategy was Ulysses S. Grant's personal memoirs, considered to be one of the best accounts of war. When Grant describes the Civil War battles, most of his description is devoted to explaining the lay of the land. The book contains numerous hand drawn maps of the battlefields. He studied the land fastidiously to determine where to position his men and how to orchestrate a battle. As the battle took place, he usually had to abandon his original plan, but knowing the lay of the land helped him devise a new course of action. This, plus his attention to logistics and supply, is how Grant won the Civil War.

Another famous, winning general was Dwight D. Eisenhower. I often refer to one of his famous quotes, "In preparing for battle I have always found that plans are useless, but planning is indispensable." Battles rarely go according to plan. Neither does life. Needless to say, businesses rarely proceed according to plan either.

The problem is that people have been sold on the strategic plan as the answer. The plan itself has very little value. As our famous military generals advised, it is the planning that adds the value. Learning about trends, economic scenarios, competitors' strengths and weaknesses, regulatory changes, and consumer feedback adds insight and wisdom to a company's decision making. With this knowledge, businesses are better able to react to situations and recognize good opportunities. Planning expands thinking while following a plan limits thinking. And the whole point of developing a strategy is to improve intelligence, not replace it! Exacerbating the problem, most companies use consultants to do the analyses and develop the plans, and all that knowledge walks out the door when the consultants are done. Instead of insight built within the company, what's left behind is a seventy-five-page PowerPoint document that few read, let alone comprehend, and that becomes obsolete almost as soon as it's printed. There is a huge difference in what you learn from spending weeks doing an analysis, documenting findings, and formulating conclusions and what you get from reading a report.

The goal of strategy development should not be a plan. Strategy development is actually a vision quest. Vision quests are not attempts to predict the future or create a plan of action but are acts of self-discovery. Strategy development should be an act of corporate self-discovery. Hence, the value of developing strategy is not in the paper document left behind. You can probably throw that away. The value is in the learning and discovery process. The goal shouldn't be to develop a plan to follow but to gain the wisdom to react appropriately to a *rapidly* changing world given the capabilities of the company. This way, when opportunities present themselves, employees can distinguish the good ones from the not-so-good ones. The problem with a plan is that it can never account for all the unplanned opportunities that will arise. And some of those unplanned opportunities will be the key to succeeding in the future. Businesses don't succeed by predicting the future and dictating the marketplace; they succeed by recognizing good opportunities and pursuing them, especially when no one else does. This is how Microsoft, Apple, and Google became market leaders, not by predicting the future, but by recognizing and seizing upon good opportunities. Logically, then, the best way to succeed is to persuade your competitors to develop and execute strategic plans while you just keep your eyes open for good opportunities.

To choose good opportunities, corporate discovery needs to include as many people as feasible. A company is the sum of its people, and how do you discover who you are if you include only the head but not the heart and soul? Most companies develop their strategies with a select few, usually the leadership team, who aren't close to customers or competitors or trends. This is how blockbuster drugs and total business transformation become strategic goals. In contrast, military leaders are constantly gathering intelligence from the field. Similarly, employees can provide a wealth of intelligence about the marketplace, customers, and even competitors—someone has probably worked there. Sharing information throughout the organization about the company's values and capabilities, projects that worked and didn't work, what customers want, and emerging technologies is all critical to good decision making. People need to know these to recognize good opportunities. This is what strategy development is really about—providing the foundation for making informed decisions. It is not about a few people making those decisions in advance.

We need to think about corporate strategy in realistic terms. Not everyone can be the market leader. Not all businesses will grow at double-digit rates or be the stars. Predicting the future is pretty much impossible even for the smartest people in the world and certainly impossible for a bunch of twenty-something-year-old consultants. However, discovering a purpose and creating the wisdom needed to make decisions about unexpected events is foolproof in comparison.

2

Make Sure You Reengineer the People, Too

Optimized Processes Only Look Good on Paper

▷ **Having people to rely on for improvements is all you really need**

Process reengineering, and with it, process automation, is where I've spent a good chunk of my career. This was the type of work I did when I began consulting, only we called it "operations improvements" before the term "process reengineering" was coined. Although my memories of many client projects all those years ago are a blur, I do remember my first client engagement well because it taught me a great deal about business problems. The client was a small refrigerator manufacturer that was suffering from excess inventory, long lead times, and an inability to meet customer orders. The business had changed over the years from just a few products to a wide-ranging product line that offered customers their choice of features and even some custom designs. The complexity of the operations had increased while the plant configuration had stayed the same. My manager had sold the client very expensive, cutting-edge software to improve its scheduling ability, a large investment for a company of this size. He had promised the software would optimize the company's plant floor and dramatically improve its production volume. Unfortunately, after following his advice and implementing the software, the company saw only slight improvements. This became a big client satisfaction issue, especially because the company was a client of other services our consulting firm offered, and the partner in charge of the manufacturing practice had to fly out and try to smooth the situation over. The result was that my manager was effectively banned from the client's site, and we offered to perform a free analysis of the company's operations and write a requirements definition for an integrated manufacturing, inventory, and financial information system. Eventually, this system would solve the company's problems because it would integrate its operations.

I found myself at this manufacturer with two accounting consultants who were going to write the requirements for the financial part. They had an office upstairs with the accounting function, while I was a given a space right above the shop floor. Because we weren't making money on this project and were unlikely to sell any follow-on, the local management basically left us to our own devices. Here I was about twelve months out of college with an engineering degree in electronic materials with absolutely no knowledge of a manufacturing enterprise, trying to solve the company's problems on my own. Although I was sold as an engineering graduate of MIT (Massachusetts Institute of Technology), my degree was in semiconductors, working at the atomic level with electron microscopes, not exactly the kind of engineering used on a shop floor. (Maybe at a much, much smaller manufacturer!)

I began my analysis with a tour of the shop floor with the supervisor. The first thing I noticed was that there were parts everywhere. Officially called "work in process," these were unfinished items making their way through the production process. Every machine had two queues of parts—coming in and going out. Because of this, the place was cluttered and filthy. Secondly, every machine operator was busy punching away at a machine. Finally, I noticed several men, better dressed and cleaner than the machine operators, walking around the floor and haggling with the operators. Every time one of these men approached a machine, the operator stopped, and the two appeared to engage in an argument. I asked the shop floor supervisor what these men were doing. He explained that they were expediters. The job of expediters was to take care of rush or high-priority orders by babysitting them all the way through production. An expediter would bring a rush order to the first machine, make sure the first part was produced, bring it to the second machine, and so on until the order was complete. Unfortunately, this process was incredibly disruptive to the production schedule, especially since it had been optimized with expensive software. Each operator had to stop what he was doing, which was making a part for an order, to retool the machine and make the part for the expediter—no wonder the software wasn't working! After the tour, I started talking with shop floor workers and production schedulers and anyone else who would talk to me. Although I was warned that the workers were "union" and likely to be uncooperative, I found that most were more than happy to talk to me, and some even vented all their frustrations with the situation, being grateful for the opportunity to be heard. Their own management was so busy that they never had time to go down to the floor and talk with anyone.

The company's procedure to create a manufacturing schedule was to require its customers to submit their orders by the end of the month. The orders were then entered into the computer, which spat out an optimized production schedule for the next month. However, the company had several important customers who submitted orders weekly that needed to be filled as soon as possible. At first, these orders were fed into the computer system and a new schedule was created, but because the old schedule was already underway, creating a new schedule with every new order became disruptive. So the new orders were kept separate and handled by expediters. Though in theory the schedule was kept intact, in practice it wasn't being followed by workers, who had to halt what they were doing to accommodate the expediters' requests. As more orders fell behind their commitment dates, more orders were designated "rush" and required expediting, with the result being that the shop floor became less optimized and fewer orders got shipped on time—a vicious circle.

After a few weeks of mostly talking with the employees, I developed a list of their problems with some recommendations. Even though I was told specifically that human resources (HR) was outside the scope of my analysis, the biggest problem was that the workers were compensated by the number of pieces produced and not by meeting the schedule. This meant that if a machine operator had to change the tools on his machine, which took about two hours, to make five pieces, which took about thirty minutes, he would make more than five parts to compensate for the changeover time. The extras would sit at the workstation and, with any luck, be found when that part was needed again. Making the situation worse, the machine operators would always appease the expediters first before following the schedule because the expediters were breathing down their necks. Again, the operators would make more than one part if they had to change tools. Finally, they would look at the schedule and see how much of that they could accomplish before the end of the day.

All the workers knew that this approach was contrary to meeting their order commitments, but this was how the floor operated. They had incentive compensation based on the number of pieces produced, so they were going to produce as many as they could, even if those pieces weren't needed. Worse, making these unnecessary pieces consumed the raw materials that were ordered for required pieces, so the operators were always running out of raw materials. This meant that the purchasing department had to order more than the schedule required, which only allowed the operators to make even more unnecessary parts. The net result was a complete disaster—lots of unsellable inventory, few completed orders, and a scarcity of raw materials.

Obviously, my first recommendation was to stop compensating employees based on the number of pieces produced and to move to on-time order fulfillment as a collective goal. I also recommended that the company get rid of the expediters and move to a weekly production schedule because customers were sending in their orders on a weekly basis anyway. It doesn't matter how nice the optimized monthly schedule looks on paper. If your customers are sending in orders every week and you are incorporating those orders into your schedule, then you are actually working from a weekly schedule. The monthly paper schedule is just pretend. I also made some recommendations for changing the order lead times and creating a separate job shop. I wish I could say that the company implemented these changes, improved its ability to ship orders, lowered its inventory and production costs, and became immensely profitable. However, after I wrote the report and presented it to management, I went on to another assignment. The president and his team seemed pleased with the recommendations, but a year later the company was bought by a larger appliance maker without having implemented much of anything.

Although at first I was a little resentful of having to work on my own at my first client, it forced me to rely on the employees for all my information and on myself to think things through. Normally, I wouldn't have had the chance to talk with so many people or spend lots of time "just thinking." In consulting, where you are rated on your ability to hit the ground running, thinking is often considered a non-value-adding activity. What I deliberated on was that, contrary to the advice that the union employees would be unhelpful and even dishonest, I found that most of them knew exactly what the problems were and wanted to help, but not only were they powerless to change the way things worked, they were alienated. The relationship between the employees on the shop floor and the management team was hostile. All it took was one painful labor contract negotiation, and the mutual mistrust soured the relationship permanently. The whole time I was there, I never saw anyone from management on the shop floor, and the workers certainly never volunteered information to their supervisors. Each painted the other as evil, greedy, uncaring, and stupid, and each used the one or two exceptions of purely self-interested people on the other side to define everyone else. Some of the human resources policies were meant to deal with these exceptions, but unfortunately, they applied to everyone else as well. What I found frustrating was that people rarely spoke to others outside their areas, and I often found myself acting as a communications vehicle. Another thing I found very frustrating was "scope creep." My manager had warned me to stick to the manufacturing operations and avoid the common consulting pitfall of scope creep, but many of the problems had their causes outside the manufacturing area. The incentive system was the root of many of the evils, but the lack of information sharing and poor relationships with customers and suppliers also created shop floor problems. I discovered that some purchasing departments would create duplicate orders at different facilities to get product faster and then cancel what they didn't need. To really fix the shop floor, you would have to include everyone else in the supply chain.

▷ **People should manage the methods and not the methods manage the people**

Over the next few years, I spent most of my time improving operations at small manufacturers using some of the methods that were popular then: bottleneck analysis using Eliyahu Goldratt's theory of constraints, just-in-time (JIT) manufacturing practices from Japan, or MRPII (manufacturing resource planning, the precursor to ERP, or enterprise resource planning) information systems. The funny thing is, none of these methods ever worked perfectly. We always had to adapt. Often manufacturers had multiple bottlenecks that needed to be addressed together rather than one by one. While some JIT principles can be applied, the reality is that you can't implement pure JIT in this country. Japan is a small country where the suppliers are never that far away. It makes no sense in the United States to try to turn all your inventory in one or two days when it takes two weeks to get raw materials. The same thing was true about implementing manufacturing software. We would never just go in and install software. We always made sure that the processes and information were correct first. Otherwise, you would have a disaster. Even then, the initial implementation usually uncovered more bad data. Based on my experiences, I thought of these methods as guidelines or tools to be used at one's discretion—the more tools you knew, the better equipped you could be.

At the time, quality initiatives were popular, and I decided to pursue a certification in statistical process control (SPC). Manufacturing automation was becoming sophisticated enough to monitor the multitude of variables in a manufacturing process such as temperature, pressure, and speed. The idea was to monitor all these variables to determine what specifications would ensure the quality of the product. Using performance histories and statistics, you could predict when a machine would likely go out of specification or if a problem was due to operator error. It was an incredible boon to manufacturing quality and productivity. SPC supplied the underpinnings of the Six Sigma movement.

The Six Sigma movement began at Motorola in the mid-1980s when the CEO and a team of engineers realized that their product quality was terrible, and they needed to drastically improve to compete with the Japanese. "Six Sigma" is a statistical reference meaning six standard deviations from the process norm. For high quality, process variations from the desired specification need to be at the six sigma range. Six sigma means only 3.4 defects per million. Typically, people think that 99 percent accuracy is good. However, this means that for every one hundred parts you make, you have one that is defective—not a high quality process. Motorola made huge strides in improving quality and reducing costs using Six Sigma, and both GE and Allied Signal jumped on the Six Sigma bandwagon and mandated it throughout their organizations. Of course, during Jack Welch's tenure, any program at GE was considered a business best practice and adopted wholesale throughout the business community. This time period also saw the rise of "business process reengineering." The term is credited to Michael Hammer, who with James Champy wrote a book called *Reengineering the Corporation*, which became a business best seller. They defined process reengineering as "the fundamental rethinking and radical redesign of business processes to achieve dramatic improvements in critical contemporary measures of performance such as cost, quality, services, and speed." Soon everyone wanted process reengineering.

I joined Gemini Consulting during this process reengineering heyday. One of the unique features of Gemini's history was that its methods were based on the work of behavioral psychologists. On each of our engagements we spent a great deal of time on "soft skills," working with our clients on how to build teams, provide coaching and feedback, and run effective meetings. Each consultant was required to learn several of what many of us number-crunchers called "touchy-feely" techniques, including a team brainstorming method, an emotional cycle-of-change model, meeting facilitation interventions, and a process reengineering tool called "brown papers." Brown papers were called that because we prepared high-level process flowcharts of the existing processes on a large roll of brown butcher paper. Then we invited all those involved in the business process to add their comments on the process using sticky notes and to elaborate on what was broken. These sessions were incredibly cathartic. We billed the method as "high touch and low tech."

This method was in stark contrast to the Six Sigma statistical basis, and being an engineer by education, I was skeptical. However, the brown papers were effective. Many of the people commenting on the papers worked in different functional areas and never had the opportunity to talk about what was broken. I found that people needed to vent before they could move on, and venting via sticky notes allowed them to air their worst vitriol without getting personal. It was the process that was broken, not the people working it. There was huge value in getting all those people in a room to discuss why they did what they did, how it impacted people elsewhere, and generally understand the problems that others faced. People walked out of the sessions with a much bigger and more human perspective of the process. There was now a face to the hated customer service representative who had to deal with frustrated customers all day long, and there was a person behind the incompetent inventory manager who had the impossible job of working with constantly outdated information. This venting and humanizing process was the first step to getting the team to work together to create something better. Although we usually had assistants create electronic versions of the brown papers to give the clients for reference, I never used them. The flowcharts weren't the product; the comments were.

After this catharsis, the next step was to get many of the same people in the room and work on the "To Be" process. I was always uncomfortable with this step because it consisted of starting with a blank piece of paper and brainstorming and questioning how to be better. Gemini always required multiple consultants at these types of meetings because you needed someone to expertly facilitate the group and someone to challenge the level of thinking—a process person and a content person. I was the kind of consultant who always liked to have the answer in my pocket, even if I didn't share it, but the point of this method was to start with a blank slate. Even though I was uncomfortable with it, it always worked. Once, I tried using a structured approach based on desired outcomes, but we found it inhibited our thinking and scrapped it after thirty minutes. Somehow the teams always created a new and improved process. Sometimes it was radically different and sometimes not so much, but whenever we left the client after implementing the new process, we always left a team of people who had formed good relationships and whose job responsibilities included continuous improvement. This simple method was incredibly effective, and Gemini became well-known for process reengineering. We were even on the cover of *BusinessWeek*.

As we became more successful and the economy dipped into a severe recession, our engagements became larger, and we started our pursuit of business transformation. In our rapid growth phase, our leadership also pushed for more intellectual property, and thought leadership became one of our rated competencies. We wanted to compete with the likes of McKinsey, and to do so, we would need to become more analytical and systematic in our approach. Other companies were developing proprietary methods and tools and using automation, and we looked like amateurs with our brown papers. We started to develop comprehensive methodologies in all our service areas as part of the business transformation strategy. At the same time, we changed the type of people we were recruiting. One of Gemini's differentiators was that our consultants came from diverse backgrounds, and many came from the industry. Now we were hiring straight out of brand-name business schools like our competitors. We started moving away from the touchy-feely approaches to more analytical tools.

It was on a large transformation engagement where I had my worst consulting experience ever. We had teams of people working at numerous sites to improve the manufacturing and supply chain at a textile manufacturer. Because of the size of the engagement and the promised quick turnaround, each functional area of the supply chain was its own project. Instead of an end-to-end process, we would have to fit the pieces together. I was assigned to a small plant on my own where my task was to reengineer the scheduling function. The situation was very similar to my first client experience—the factory was unable to fill its orders on a timely basis and had lots of angry customers. When the plant was built, the industry had much more demand than supply, and this plant took all the rejected spools of thread from the other sites and respooled the product onto much larger spools that fit on weaving machines. This way the plant could sell initially rejected product to get more revenues. However, the nature of the industry had changed, and the plant was now making lots of customized spools with different sizes, thread counts, and so on. In short, over the years, the product line had become very complex. An initial consulting assessment had promised a vast increase in machine uptime and hence significantly larger throughput. Instead of expensive software to solve the plant's problems, we were offering process reengineering.

Left to my own devices, I did what I usually do—I toured the facility and interviewed the employees. The problem was pretty obvious. There were about twenty huge spooling machines. On one end, a worker placed about a hundred small spools of thread on spindles and then manually threaded the machine that wound the thread onto the big spools. It often took days for a worker to thread one machine, and some of the runs lasted only a few hours. Many of the machines were idle because they were being threaded or because they had a complicated setup and were waiting for an order with that particular setup. To make matters worse, because the plant was built to repurpose rejected spools, many of the spools of raw material were only partial, and the workers were continually shutting the machines down to restring new thread. To say this was a labor-intensive operation is a huge understatement.

Like the refrigerator manufacturer, this client had sophisticated scheduling software, but its customers frequently changed their orders. The customers served fashion houses, which reserved the right to change their orders on a whim because that's just how the fashion business is. Demand changes rapidly. Ideally, the client wanted customers to send their orders in monthly so that the schedulers could enter the orders into the software to create an optimized monthly schedule. The schedulers were constantly trying to protect the monthly schedule, while their customers were constantly trying to change it to meet changing demand. This meant the machines were constantly down. At the other sites, where chemicals were poured in one end and thread came out the other, improving maintenance and machine schedules would improve the uptime; however, this was not the case here. The problem was much bigger. It wasn't the process that was broken; it was the business model. When the plant was built and the product was more expensive, the labor costs were much lower, and only a few types of spools were sold. It made sense to retool the rejected spools into something sellable. In the current world, where the product was more widely available and the margins were much lower, it made little sense. Now every spool cost more to make than it was sold for. Gemini had promised that we could lower the plant's manufacturing costs by increasing its uptime as if it were a process plant like all the others.

As soon as I understood that improving the scheduling algorithm would have little impact, I called the project manager to tell him the situation. Getting the schedulers and workers together to work on "As Is" brown papers didn't seem to have much point. The plant had a small staff who were well aware of the problems but were powerless to address them. The problem was with the relationships with the customers—mainly one customer who was responsible for at least half the orders and most of the changes, so we decided that we would visit the customer. I organized a daylong meeting where teams from the client and the customer could start to address the problem together. People from both companies took turns discussing their problems and, in a nonthreatening way, their frustrations with each other. We spent the morning venting and getting to know each other on a professional level. We ate lunch together and started to learn about each other on a personal level. During the lunch, the customer team admitted that sometimes they ordered more than they needed to ensure that they would get enough product. At first, my client was furious that they were trying to optimize phony orders. I chimed in that I'd seen this practice at other companies, and others in the room admitted that this was common. This little confession set the tone for very candid communications.

In the afternoon, I led the teams through a structured brainstorming session, where we developed lots of ideas on how to work together better. After fully immersing ourselves in each others' problems, we tried to generate ideas that would help both companies. At the end of the day, we left with a list of possible solutions and actions to find out how we could make them work. One of the suggestions was to let the customer schedule some of the machines and take responsibility for determining which orders to fill first, and another was to provide spooling as a service rather than as a product, where the plant would sell the customer the time and labor involved. Then it wouldn't have to struggle to optimize throughput. We walked away from the meeting with a new understanding and some hope for finding a way to work together better. I was very pleased that we had moved beyond the "blame game" and now had the beginnings of a fruitful relationship.

When I returned to the plant, the project manager had been reassigned, and a whole new consulting team was now working there. Apparently, my alert that I would probably not deliver the promised benefits set a whole chain of events in motion. It was deemed that the challenge was too much for one consultant, and an entire team who had worked at another site was brought in. At this time, Gemini was starting to standardize its service offering and its methodologies. This team had brought tools and solutions from the other sites, and they were going to use them to do a full diagnostic and repair. The first thing that my new manager asked to see was my documentation for the As Is scheduling process. I explained the situation and that I really didn't see the point in documenting the current scheduling process. He was quite furious with me for going way out of scope and for not following our standardized process. That was why I couldn't find the benefits. I was directed to immediately stop what I was doing and to create the process flowchart. A little at a loss because I was unable to explain the real problems at the plant, I embarked on the As Is process, which consisted of about four steps: send orders-due reminders to customers, input the orders into state-of-the-art scheduling software at month-end, print an optimized monthly schedule and send it to the floor supervisors, and revise the schedule as new orders arrive. The last step had a loop back into the previous one.

When I showed this to the manager, he was again furious. What kind of documentation was this? Clearly, I was incompetent. He asked another consultant to show me what a scheduling brown paper was supposed to look like and to show me the tools I needed to use to develop the new process. The problem was, these tools and solutions were for simple process plants that had only a few products. This manager had yet to tour the plant or talk with the employees, but already he had the solutions because they had been successful at other plants. I was incredulous at his insistence that if I did the documentation correctly, the problems would be solved. When I was equally as insistent that these tools wouldn't work, I was asked to leave the project. Normally, this is a consulting career ender, but I already had some other successes under my belt, so I was given another chance. I switched from supply-chain processes to new product development, where I had more leeway to use my judgment. Eventually, it became well-known that that project was a disaster, and the partner who ran it was let go a year later. The manufacturer never realized the promised benefits at that facility, and it was eventually sold. (Are you sensing a trend?)

This was an incredibly disheartening experience for me. After meeting with the customer and having that brainstorming session, I saw a glimmer of hope that maybe there could be a solution for this client. I felt like I had actually helped someone. When I was forced to follow the recommended process rather than use my own judgment, I went to work sick to my stomach every day. I knew what I was doing was wrong. I had always used methods and tools as a means to an end, not as an end itself. I always thought the point of these methodologies was to supply new insights and challenge conventional thinking. My colleagues and I never saw them as step-by-step recipes for success. What was great about Gemini when I joined was that all of our methods were excuses for getting people to work together better. Now they had become a substitute for getting people to work together better.

▷ In a human-created world, most of the problems are created by humans

The irony is that if you go back to the book that started it all, *Reengineering the Corporation*, the authors purposely recommend that to be successful, you need to get everyone involved in the solution. They also specifically state that there is no step-by-step method for developing new processes. They recommend starting from a blank slate. The last chapter or two of almost every business book today is an instruction guide on how to implement the solution correctly. What I really like about *Reengineering the Corporation* is that rather than ending with a recipe, the authors discuss some of the situations where reengineering initiatives have gone wrong. They also have a very useful chapter on typical symptoms of process problems, like data redundancy being a symptom of process fragmentation and inventory buffers being used to deal with uncertainty. The difference between offering an instruction manual and describing mistakes and problems is that the former limits thinking while the latter expands it.

In contrast, Six Sigma starts not with a blank slate but with the current process, and many critics of this methodology complain that it offers incremental improvement and not anything radical or innovative. I think most people are missing the big picture. Six Sigma is a control process that has its origins in machine control. This is great when you are working with equipment, but what about when you are working with people? I have a reference book for implementing Six Sigma for marketing processes, and it is full of templates for monitoring task completion and documenting stage-gate criteria. The point of these templates is to instill discipline and consistency into marketing processes. Why would I hire smart, creative, psychologically savvy people and have them spend their time filling out document templates and monitoring progress in minute detail when they should be brainstorming new product ideas and new marketing campaigns? Isn't the marketing function supposed to be chaotic?

Years ago I used to teach problem-solving tools to other consultants. Figure 1 shows one of the tools that is part of the Six Sigma toolkit, an Ishikawa or fishbone diagram, used to identify root causes.

Causes for a Car Not to Start

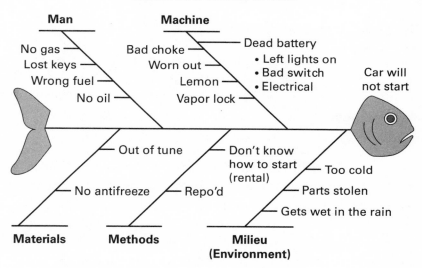

Figure 1 **Fishbone diagram**

The car example above bothered me for years, and I often searched for a better one but never found one I liked. Eventually, I realized that the problem wasn't with the example but with the tool itself. We have five possible categories of causes for the car not starting—man, machine, materials, methods, and milieu. The most obvious answer is that it's a dead battery, a machine problem, but if you ask why the battery is dead, it's from leaving the lights on—ultimately a human problem. Take a look at the methods and the materials categories. The car is out of tune, has no antifreeze, or has been repossessed or the driver doesn't know how to start it—these are really human problems. In fact, pretty much all business problems are human problems. Even many manufacturing equipment problems are really human problems, caused by operator error or poor maintenance. In a human-created world, it is hard to find a problem that isn't ultimately created by a human.

▷ It's hard to optimize a person

I have spent at least a decade reengineering processes and finding root causes, and I have discovered several that appear over and over again in process problems. I have never seen these discussed in the reengineering literature:

• *Mistrust*—This is probably the biggest problem in broken processes. When people work in silos and don't communicate, they don't understand why their counterparts in other departments are doing the crazy stuff they do. This misunderstanding sets in motion all sorts of games, controls, cross-checking, and review and approval steps, none of which add value. Mistrust, along with fear and hope, is the fundamental cause of the notorious supply-chain bullwhip effect, where small deviations in demand ripple through the chain and become huge deviations at the end. Basically, customers are bumping up their orders because they don't trust that their suppliers will deliver, and this continues along the whole chain of customers and suppliers. When customers do get their demand filled, they cancel the rest of their orders, which again ripples down the chain. This leads to a cycle of over- and undersupply situations.

• *Conflicting goals/working at odds*—I'll talk more about this cause in the next chapter, but basically, functional silos often have goals that conflict with other functions' goals. For instance, Sales wants absolutely no stockouts while Inventory Management is working on decreasing inventory levels; Marketing wants to launch a product quickly while Regulatory insists on extensive product quality checks; headquarters wants to reduce the number of internal initiatives while the regions are running improvement programs that spawn lots of new initiatives. These are just a small sample of the examples I've encountered.

• *Impatience*—This impacts almost every initiative and project undertaken at a company and is becoming more and more of a problem with the rapid pace of work. Most often I see this in new product development when an important new product or a pet project is on the docket and people can't wait to get started—literally. Unfortunately, stuffing a project pipeline full actually clogs it up. People can work on only a few projects at a time, and starting numerous projects at the same time means none of them get completed. I also see this happen with many corporate initiatives. Impatient to get going, the project team skips the proper analysis to determine the actual causes of their problems and ends up implementing solutions that make matters worse.

• *Fear of looking foolish*—This is a big problem in new product development. Often, the members of the group working on a new product want to perfect their concept before they share it with anyone else. Unfortunately, what happens is that after spending months perfecting the concept, they discover that it is unviable from a legal or regulatory or manufacturing perspective. They've wasted all that time working on an idea that could never launch. Putting incomplete concepts out to everyone involved means you can weed out the bad ones faster, but no one wants to appear foolish.

What I would like to know is which process optimization software and which reengineering methodology deals with these issues? I'd also like to see the flowchart that solves these problems. Like our pretend optimized monthly schedule, these process flows look great on paper but often don't represent the reality of the situation. A big part of this problem is the belief that work processes are separate from people. People do the work and are the work process. For instance, when I was streamlining a new product development process, the senior vice president in charge of development wanted insight into all the product concepts, so we put in an approval step at the beginning. During the project, he left the company, and his replacement didn't want to see product concepts until later in the process, so the approval step was taken out.

The idea behind all this analysis and documentation and charting is that this discipline will uncover the roots of your business problems. However, the best things about human-based problems are that we are self-aware and we can communicate. We can tell you what's wrong, but you do have to ask. In my experience, for the majority of business problems, at least one person knows exactly what is causing it. If not, partial knowledge of the cause resides in multiple heads, and you need to bring them together to get the full problem. These root cause and problem-solving tools are effective when you bring people together who normally don't have a chance to communicate with each other. The tools by themselves are pretty useless. Using a tool or a methodology or a piece of software as an excuse to hold a meeting or kick off a cross-functional team is an effective problem-solving method. People like to use tools. That's how we evolved into a civilization. The caution is thinking that the tool holds the solution and can be effective without bringing the people together, and unfortunately, that's how many of these methodologies evolve. They start out as people-based techniques, and then someone decides to eliminate the messy human variable. The next thing you know, you have a data- and documentation-heavy methodology that requires an inordinate amount of time for consulting analysts to complete, and if they are lucky, their analyses will stumble upon the right answer. But all that effort could have been used to just ask the people involved and to work on the problem together in a creative and collaborative way. Yet we don't have time to work on process problems together because we are too busy inputting data, documenting flowcharts, installing software, analyzing data, and creating reports to do any meaningful improvement work.

Documents, reports, and plans are not the real deliverables. As with strategic plans, the value is in the thinking, learning, and creating and not in the resulting paperwork. The document will be obsolete before you print it anyway. Any tool, method, program, or initiative that promises to solve your business problems without including everyone involved in your business problem will fail. Whether it is a software program or change initiative, the only way to improve your operations is to get all your people together to work on them. Then it doesn't really matter what tool or methodology you choose. Your people are both the problem and the solution.

3

Metrics Are the Means, Not the Ends

Numerical Targets Are Measure-mental

▷ **Everything gets measured all the time**

Because of the obsession with financial measures that arose in the 1980s, someone was bound to note that it takes more than just managing the financials to run a business. Those someones were Robert Kaplan and David Norton, who published a paper on the balanced scorecard (BSC) in the *Harvard Business Review (HBR)* in 1992. The premise of the BSC is that four categories of measures are needed to manage a business successfully—financial, customer satisfaction, internal processes, and innovation and learning. Ideally, the measures in these four categories would be determined by the business's strategic goals, and the scorecard could be used to operationalize a strategic plan. The BSC would include both internal and external objectives for implementing the strategy with numerical targets that would let you know your progress. See figure 2 for an example.

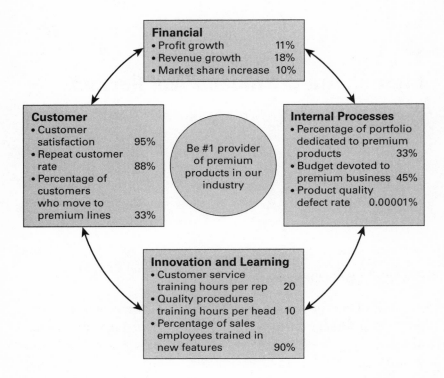

Figure 2 **Balanced scorecard**

This BSC aligns an organization around creating premium products with the purpose of improving profits, revenues, and market share with those as the designated financial measures with end-of-year targets. The other categories help operationalize the strategy: process goals include the number of premium products in development, percentage of budget devoted to premium products, and defect rate; customer goals include satisfaction rate, retention, and percentage who purchase the premium lines; and learning goals include customer service training hours and R&D training budget. (There are no innovation goals in this example.) All these measures contribute to achieving the premium provider market leader status as the strategy.

However, if the BSC was going to help implement a new strategy, it didn't go far enough. High-level objectives are fine for the C suite, but how do the workers contribute to market share or training budget goals? The next logical step was called "key performance indicators" (KPIs). Each of the balanced scorecard measures could be broken down into its component measures—for instance, revenue consists of sales volume and price. Each of those measures could be further broken down and then the resulting measures also broken down. For example, total sales is broken down into country sales and then into regional sales; price is broken down into unit cost and profit margin (see figure 3). This process of breaking down metrics into a hierarchy of component measures was sometimes called "cascading" key performance indicators. This way, every level in the organization could contribute to implementing the strategy and achieving the strategic objectives. As a machine operator or customer service representative, I could see how my role contributed to the overall objectives through the use of this hierarchy of submetrics.

We consultants took to this measurement system like remoras to a shark. The problem with most consulting at the time was that the firms did the analysis, developed the strategy or new process, created a recommended implementation plan, and

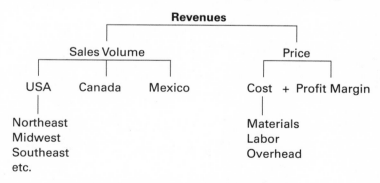

Figure 3 **Cascading key performance indicators**

then left for another client. Executing the strategy was left to the client. The process work helped but often didn't cover all the strategic objectives, and it was up to the client's management team to enforce both the new processes and the new strategic plan. One doesn't make much money in consulting by trusting managers to do their jobs well. If they did, they wouldn't need us. Now we had tools to monitor the implementation and results of our efforts.

With the balanced scorecard, we could break the strategy down into strategic objectives in the four areas and add targets. Combined with new work processes, this system of measures was a surefire method of implementing the strategy. In this way, how each person in the organization contributed to the strategic objectives could be monitored and measured. It provided discipline to the messy business of organizational change. This structure was wonderfully appealing to both consultants and clients alike. The result would be an entire company aligned around specific goals and targets, with everyone able to measure how well she is doing her part—a complete command-and-control system for implementing strategic objectives. Even better, consultants could sell the balanced scorecard and cascading key performance indicators as a stand-alone service.

Pretty much every consulting project I've been involved with over the last two decades has had some metrics component. The use of metrics for any kind of project is so widespread that people rarely ever question the value of collecting and monitoring measurements. It's a given that you need a system of measures to accomplish anything. The following two points are from a PowerPoint presentation I have often used in client engagements that seem to be a mainstay in pretty much every consultant's repertoire:

You can't manage what you can't measure!

A metrics scorecard acts like a car's dashboard.
Executives monitor progress with large meters and are
notified of problems when small warning lights turn red.

The rise of information technology during this same period made the data collection and reporting needed for this whole measurement and monitoring system much easier to implement. It started with executive dashboards that showed progress toward key metrics. Then IT worked its way into employee performance appraisals with the development of automated performance management systems driven by SMART (specific, measurable, actionable, results-oriented, and time-bound) goals and metrics that linked upward and downward. As executive dashboards became popular, businesses wondered why they should be limited to executives, and with web technologies, any employee or department could have its own dashboard to monitor measures. These web pages look a lot like the control panels used to monitor machines, with red alerts, yellow caution signals, and green icons meaning "on-track." Now executives and managers could see exactly what was going on without ever having to leave their desks or talk with anyone. They could manage everything with a simple, color-coded web interface. Just like statistical process control, it was a perfect command-and-control system with warnings whenever any of the measures went "off-spec." What could possibly be wrong with that?

▷ It's funny how the targets are always met

The problem is that the system is trying to command and control an organization composed of people. And the problem with people is that, well, we're people. We don't operate like machinery. In fact, we really don't like being commanded or controlled, and our reactions to these measurement systems cause our behaviors to change in unpredictable ways. One thing I have learned from these measurement systems is that if you pick a specific goal and attach rewards and punishments to it, you can pretty much guarantee that somehow that goal will be met. Unfortunately, this often comes at the expense of other worthy, but nonmeasured, business goals. The most straightforward example, and the place where numerical targets got their start, is in sales organizations. Today, most companies have moved away from paying their sales representatives straight salaries to offering commission-based compensation, that is, the more a person sells, the more he makes. Typically, a salesperson has quarterly revenue targets to meet to get the incentive compensation. Anyone familiar with sales knows that sales usually pick up at the end of each quarter and then drop off at the beginning. This is because salespeople offer promotions and other incentives, like rebates, to their customers to order before the close of the quarter. Of course, promotions and rebates harm profitability, but most salespeople aren't measured on profits, so they don't care.

Sales representatives often game the system to their advantage. Probably the worst example I have ever seen was when a regional manager got fed up with the unachievable revenue targets he was given every year. Not only did he not get a bonus, but all the members of his team were penalized in their compensation. It's one thing to suffer the penalty yourself, but having to inform the hardworking people on your staff year after year that they didn't make the cut can be heart wrenching. One year, he persuaded his distributors to buy more product than they wanted so he and his team could meet their year-end sales goals. He promised that they could return what they didn't sell. He and his team met their targets and got their bonuses, and the company was flooded with returns two quarters later. (He had already planned his resignation.) Besides having to write off most of this product, a huge cost, the company also had to pay for the extra handling and storage and the bad will that resulted from this scheme. Of course, in this manager's defense, the sales targets he was asked to meet had no grounding in reality but were the result of an executive's desire for double-digit growth in a stagnant market. Somewhere at the root of this thinking was a consultant's advice that stretch goals would spark creativity in meeting them. (I used to say this. I'm sorry.) They certainly did!

The games people play in meeting their targets are widely documented in business literature. Here is just a small sampling of examples:

• Perhaps the most famous case is the Sears auto repair scandal. The state of California charged Sears auto centers with fraud after Sears instituted incentive compensation schemes based on sales targets for certain parts and services. The result was that customers had unnecessary repairs done on their cars without their consent or knowledge. Needless to say, the company's business suffered as a result of the customer fraud.

• *Reengineering the Corporation* relates an anecdote about the IBM credit department that had reengineered its processes and set performance standards for each step. Although it was getting 100 percent compliance with the targets, the lead time to process a credit application had actually increased. When workers were in danger of missing their volume targets, they returned bids to the senders when they found typos or other errors instead of just correcting the errors themselves.

• Among the examples Jeffrey Pfeffer writes about in an *HBR* article on pay myths is Highland Superstores. After Highland instituted commission targets for the sales staff, the resulting behavior of the salespeople was so aggressive that it alienated customers.

• Gregg Stocker, in his book *Avoiding the Corporate Death Spiral*, has identified an obsession with numbers as one of the steps in the spiral, and among the examples he gives are a public transportation authority and a post office. The transportation authority decided to align the pay of bus drivers with their on-time arrival rate. As a result, drivers skipped stops if they were running late, leaving passengers stranded. A post office that instituted targets for mail processing times found numerous bags of undelivered mail hidden away. When workers couldn't process all the mail within their targets, they just hid the mail.

• In "Paying People to Lie," Michael Jensen writes about numerous cases of deception and fraud in meeting sales targets, including a software company that was cited by the Securities and Exchange Commission for backdating sales, booking maintenance agreements as software sales, and paying fictitious consulting fees to customers in lieu of giving them product refunds.

• More recently, a federal investigation on fraud in home foreclosures cited that performance measures contributed to "robo-signing," where foreclosures were processed without being read or having the proper documentation. How many people lost their homes as well as their life savings because bank staff were under pressure to process a target number of foreclosures?

These are the worst-case examples where people resort to deception and fraud to meet targets. Not everyone will stoop so low, but I have noticed that people will often manipulate the measures to meet them. For example, as a frequent flier for most of my life, I noticed that about a decade ago, stated flight durations lengthened. This coincided with industry-wide measures of on time arrival. When I first started flying decades ago, a flight was never early. It was either on time or late. Now it is commonplace for flights to arrive thirty to forty-five minutes *early*, which initially seems like a good thing. However, if you've arranged for a ride to pick you up at the arrival time, you could be waiting around the airport for a while.

In another example, I worked for a corporate department that conducted annual customer satisfaction surveys. For years, we had shown steady improvements. After a while, our service levels plateaued. Even though the satisfaction level was still high, the leadership team was under pressure to show continuous improvement. The answer was to count all the "neither approve nor disapprove" answers on a feedback survey as positive responses, showing a nonexistent improvement over the prior year.

The reason why businesses love measures is because they mistakenly believe that measures are real, hard data. Another misguided management mantra, "The numbers don't lie," forgets that people are the ones monitoring, collecting, configuring, and reporting the measures. Measures are not objective. Measures lie all the time, even financial ones. Finance is not a science but a matter of opinion; the rules are only generally accepted accounting principles (the United States uses GAAP versus international financial reporting standards [IFRS]) and can differ from country to country. What goes into a unit cost, or a capital expenditure versus an expense, or what qualifies as an asset can vary from company to company and can be manipulated to paint the desired picture. An extreme example is the financial games Enron played.

For one client, I was asked to improve the company's manufacturing costs, which had recently ballooned. Nothing at the plant had changed except for the way overhead costs were allocated. Bundling up overhead costs and divvying them up by space occupied or by number of employees is not a true representation of what something costs. Yet most companies use some kind of overhead allocation formula because it is convenient. It takes too much time to figure out which products use the most electricity or what department consumes the most network bandwidth. What something costs is a matter of convention rather than a "hard" number. Revenues are harder to fudge, but *when* a sale is booked is a matter of convention. This can make a difference in meeting those quarterly targets.

You can play lots of games in accounting and financial reporting, and when you get to the squishier measures, there is even more room for creativity. When does the clock start on new product development cycle time—when the product is an idea or when it has a budget or when a project manager gets assigned? Are classroom supplies included in the training dollars per employee? Does defective product quantity include the pieces that were reworked to meet the specifications? See how much fun you can have? Even better, you can change the definitions every year to show improvement. Include the rework one year and exclude it the next, and, voila, defective parts show a dramatic decline! (But make sure you include a tiny footnote on the chart to document the change in measurement. You don't want to be accused of fraud!)

In reaction to all this game playing, companies often implement countermeasures. These are additional measurements that act as a balance to the original metric designed to achieve the strategic goal. Let's revisit the sales function where sales commissions are based on target revenue volumes at the expense of profit margins. The next iteration of the game includes a profitability measure. Now we have salespeople pushing the high-margin products, which seems like a good thing, except they are pushing them instead of other, cheaper products. The result is angry customers who have been bullied into buying pricier items. Annoyed, they start to buy from competitors. Or in reverse, let's add a customer satisfaction index to the mix instead of profitability. Now the salespeople have no incentive to sell products at a reasonable margin. Selling at or near cost improves both sales volumes and customer satisfaction even though it hurts the company. So the only thing that makes sense is to measure revenues, profitability, *and* customer service. Now we have increased returns! Customers are motivated to buy with a no-questions-asked-free-returns policy. So add customer returns to the mix. After a few rounds of this game, the result is a laundry list of measures and targets. The focus on and priority of the strategic objectives are gone, and the only work that gets accomplished is the measurements. Worse, long-term goals or work that isn't covered by an annual measure falls by the wayside. Any incentive to invest in the long-term future of the company is gone.

▷ Measures create conflict where there normally is none

These examples show the game playing and willful manipulation that occur in these measurement systems—a worst-case scenario. Yet even when no game playing or manipulation is involved and the people being measured are compliant—a best-case scenario— these trickle-down measurement systems do the opposite of what is intended. I learned a very interesting lesson about conflicting metrics from a big supply-chain process reengineering project. The client had typical supply-chain problems—lots of inventory, long lead times, many unfulfilled orders, and unhappy customers. A few weeks into the engagement, the flagship plant burned down, severely diminishing the amount of product, throwing everyone into a panic. Rather than continue with the project, some of the consultants were asked to help manage the crisis. During the ensuing weeks, the consultants established a process for contacting customers, negotiating orders and due dates, working with contract suppliers, and shipping to meet delivery dates. As expected, the surplus inventory was eliminated, but additionally, the lead times decreased, orders arrived as planned, customers paid earlier, and both customer satisfaction and profitability improved, albeit at reduced revenues.

The bottom line improved because the margins on the smaller sales revenues increased and the costs of carrying inventory and accounts receivables decreased. These results blew me away—all the improvements without the process reengineering. At the time, I wasn't sure why, but over the next few years, I continued to work in supply chain and eventually figured out why those large, segmented projects rarely showed the improvements we expected. Here is a typical supply chain, the typical measures, and the consequences of rewarding those measures. I am assuming no game playing occurs.

Sales—Salespeople are responsible for selling the goods and obtaining the customer orders. As I've already discussed, most sales functions have quarterly sales quotas, resulting in a big push to meet the quota at the end of quarter when it looks like it won't be met. Customers who are planning to place orders in the beginning of the next quarter are given rebates or other promotions to place them before quarter end. Besides the peak at the end of the quarter, this causes a trough at the beginning of the next quarter.

Result: Sales representatives are creating artificial spikes and troughs in demand and may be eating into profit margins with promotions. The dreaded supply-chain bullwhip effect of spikes in demand actually starts in-house.

Order entry/customer service—Each order gets processed either by a computer or by a human. Either way, the purpose of this function is to ensure the order information is correct and determine when the order can be filled. Although some companies use processing times as their metrics, most companies have learned the dangers of quantity measures (filling lots of orders quickly but incorrectly) and prefer quality metrics like order accuracy. Accuracy is important because it can be costly to fill the wrong order, process a return, and then fill it again correctly. Plus, incorrect fulfillment tends to annoy customers.

Result: Customer service representatives are incentivized to verify that all the order information is correct, erring on the side of caution and possibly double-checking with the customer or sales rep, which is at odds with minimizing the overall order lead time.

Warehouse—If product inventory is on hand, the warehouse picks the product and stages it for shipping. Inventory management is a delicate balance. Too much inventory means that lots of money is tied up in unsold product that incurs warehousing costs and risks obsolescence from sitting too long on the shelves. Too little inventory could mean stockouts, where customer orders can't be filled until more product is made, risking the loss of sales. Inventory managers typically determine how much stock to keep on hand by calculating how long it takes to make the product plus how long it takes to process an order (order lead time) and using a fudge factor based on the variability in demand. If product demand does not fluctuate much, they don't need much safety stock to cover the variation. However, if demand is irregular, they need to store enough product to cover the peaks in demand. If it takes a long time to make the product, they again need to store a lot of inventory. However, more inventory means more carrying costs and more risk of obsolescence—hence, the delicate balance. Their ideal world would be to have stable demand and short order lead times.

Result: Inventory managers are usually penalized more heavily for stockouts than for having too much on hand. They usually err on the safe side and order more inventory to cover the peaks in demand. This means warehouses typically have more product than is actually needed, prompting sales promotions later on.

Manufacturing—Factories are primarily concerned with pumping out enough product to meet demand, maintaining the quality of that product, and keeping their costs low. This means that ideally, plants want to run at or near capacity. Typically, all the plant overhead costs, like utilities and salaries, are factored into the cost of products with the result that the more you make, the lower the costs.

Result: Plant managers are measured on their machine up-time, volume of output, product costs, and quality. They want to make as much product as possible but not necessarily the right products to fill orders.

Distribution—Finally, completed orders are sent to Distribution, where they are loaded on trucks and shipped to their destinations. This function is usually measured on its freight costs. Because of this, distribution managers aim to ship full truckloads, meaning some orders may sit at the dock waiting for other orders going to the same destination. Trying to ship full loads to a variety of destinations in a timely fashion is like a puzzle, weighing the need to be on time with the need to keep costs low.

Result: To keep freight costs low, shipments wait for other shipments to the same destination. This adds to the overall lead time.

This is how the individual functions are typically measured. However, for the entire order fulfillment process, the goals and associated measurements are the number of orders that are delivered on time, the total order fulfillment lead time, and customer satisfaction. All the functional areas should be focused on filling orders as quickly and accurately as possible, yet few are measured on this. Instead, many of these functional areas are working at cross-purposes to each other. To summarize:

• Salespeople are creating artificial spikes and troughs in demand that lead to the need for more inventory to cover the variability. Salespeople hate out-of-stock situations, which means they can't make that sale so they want lots of stock on hand.

• Plant managers want to produce as much product as possible to keep the cost per unit low. This is at odds with keeping inventory levels low. Their desire to maximize machine uptime is at odds with filling orders as quickly as possible. They also don't want to bring a machine down to satisfy an order.

• Customer service wants to verify orders to ensure accuracy, but this adds to the order lead time, which means more inventory.

• Distribution wants to ship full truckloads, which also adds to the order lead time and means more inventory.

• The warehouse and anyone responsible for managing costs, like the financial group, don't want to pay the costs of storing large amounts of inventory that may become obsolete in the future.

By segmenting each function and setting up separate measures, we are motivating people to work at cross-purposes. The workers in each function are trying to maximize their own performance metric at the expense of the others. In the case of the plant fire, everyone in the supply chain became aligned around the goal of filling orders in a timely fashion. Some of the individual metrics, like distribution costs, had to be sacrificed to meet the overall goal of filling customers' orders. The crisis had inadvertently forced the company to choose which goal was most important and aligned the supply-chain organization around it.

Why are companies instituting contradictory measurements? Aren't the measurement systems supposed to be built around strategic goals? The first problem is that if everyone was measured only on meeting the delivery commitments, the other nonmeasured parameters wouldn't be managed. Manufacturing, warehousing, and distribution costs would increase, possibly beyond reason, to meet delivery and customer satisfaction goals. We would end up creating our game-playing scenario. Secondly, it's not really fair to measure and compensate people on variables beyond their control. Although customer service representatives play a key role in order fulfillment and customer satisfaction, they don't control how much inventory to store or when to make a product. Therefore, they could be doing a great job, but stockouts could prevent them from meeting their targets. If you are going to tie compensation to the achievement of measures, you have to create measures and targets that are within the functional area's control, even though they may be at odds with the company's goals.

But look at what you have ended up creating—measures that conflict with the strategic objectives and the complete loss of priorities. All the measures become equally important; therefore, none are more important than the others—the antithesis of aligning around strategic objectives. Aside from all the game playing and people working at cross-purposes, you've also created a data collection, verification, and reporting morass of measurements and targets, all of which is subject to human interpretation and manipulation. None of this work actually adds any value. It doesn't contribute to new product creation or better sales or improved operations. The net result is the same unprioritized, misaligned environment as before the metrics were instituted, plus lots of non-value-adding work administering the measurement system and minus the ability of the employees to use their own judgment to mitigate conflicting priorities.

▷ Take a goal you want and turn it into something you don't

Where my consulting colleagues and I got this whole system of cascading measures wrong is in the assumptions about how and why people work. As graduates of the best schools and general overachievers, we know that we are motivated by a job well done.

Other people, though? We just assumed that the average worker needs either a carrot or a stick or a combination of the two to work in the company's interests. The idea that other people could be motivated by achieving a goal or creating value or contributing to a team never occurred to us. Economic theories at the time stated that people behave only in their own self-interests, usually for a monetary gain. However, this can't be true. Otherwise, charities, Wikipedia, open-source software, community boards, and countless other altruistic endeavors couldn't exist. What we didn't realize was that creating the rewards and punishments based on target measures made employees self-interested at the expense of the company's interests. We motivated employees to meet the targets and nothing but the targets. The mere act of defining individual numerical targets creates a conflict with the greater organizational goals.

Our second flawed assumption, and this likely has its roots in arrogance, too, was that people would be mindfully compliant with their goals and take their punishments without fighting against the system. The expectation was that if an individual goal conflicted with a company goal, the employee would act in the greater good and use good judgment to avoid fraud or other destructive behavior. Executives were shocked when salespeople bullied their customers or bus drivers skipped stops. What happened to good judgment? Being controlled like a piece of machinery doesn't leave much room for judgment. With specific directives and targets, employees are instructed to achieve their targets without question and without exception, that is, mindlessly. The whole system is designed to remove human judgment. Without the measures, management would have to rely on employees' judgment to make the right decisions and perform the right work. Inventory managers and shipment clerks would have to balance the costs and benefits of storing more products or delaying shipments to fill a truck.

The times when I've been successful at improving supply-chain operations are the times when I got all the people together to negotiate priorities and determine what trade-offs to make. Of course, it helps if they know whether the company's over-arching goal is low cost or high customer service. But given the direction—emphasis is on direction and not directive—humans are usually able to judge what to do. Funny thing, when you remove human judgment from decision making, you get decisions that are not judicious. The point of improving operations is not to remove human judgment from the operations but to improve the human judgment that runs the operations. (Yes, sometimes that judgment needs a lot of improving.)

The important thing to realize about metrics is that they are a means, not an end. Numerical targets have been a disaster because they have supplanted the objectives the company really wants. Measures were supposed to help you manage, not become the way you manage. Tying them into incentive systems with punitive ramifications means the metrics have become the ends. The easiest way to illustrate this point is by using a weight-loss example. Most people can relate to the need to lose weight. Let's compare the goal "Lose twenty-five pounds in six months" to "Improve my overall health and fitness." Businesses would choose the time-bound, measurable goal. Yet this goal can lead to all kinds of health issues. To achieve this goal, you could diet, but afterward, you'd likely gain the weight back. If you choose to exercise, then you run the risk of gaining weight by building muscle because muscle weighs more than fat. If you aren't anywhere near your target weight at five months, you may become tempted to starve yourself. This has the harmful effect of ruining your metabolism, making you more prone to weight gain. Or you may try a more extreme form of exercising, which makes you more prone to injury.

The second goal allows you to use whatever metrics you choose—weight loss, clothing size, body mass index, miles run, weights lifted—to monitor your progress. It doesn't allow you to cheat your way to the goal by sacrificing your health, which is essentially what many short-term corporate goals do. The second goal is all about long-term lifestyle changes. And the absolutely best part about the goal is that it is not time bound nor achievable. You have to constantly work at it! You will never get there! That's what continuous improvement is all about.

The biggest irony of this whole measurement madness is that by insisting a lofty, intangible, continuous goal is unattainable and replacing it with a measurable, time-bound goal, you are actually ensuring that you will never achieve the first goal because you have replaced it with a different goal. The balanced scorecard and accompanying array of metrics don't help achieve an overarching goal; they replace the goal you want with ones that you don't. A company that wants to create new and innovative consumer electronics products will be advised to state this in measurable terms, like "create x many new and innovative products by year-end." This scenario is comparable to our weight-loss-versus-healthy-lifestyle goals—these are two completely different ends! In the second case, the most important parts of the goal are the *how many* and *by when*. The whole *new and innovative* part takes a backseat. The likely result will be a slew of new but not really innovative products—exactly the opposite of what the company wants. What bothers me most are all the corporate mission statements that seek to achieve measurable gains in market share or revenues or some other financial goal. Is that really what the management team and shareholders want? Or do they want a vital, healthy company that's going to be around for a while?

The simplest way to solve this measurement madness is to decouple the metrics from incentive compensation and any other kind of rewards and punishments. This way the goals don't have to be measurable, and the company can actually pursue the goals it really wants, not the substitute, short-term goals that meet the measurement criteria. Measures can be used to provide insight and improve knowledge, but they shouldn't be the goals themselves nor should they become the management system. Measures can't make good decisions. Only people can make good decisions. And the way to help people make good decisions is to ensure that they understand the company's overall goals and priorities and that they have the tools and knowledge to help them improve their judgment. Measurements can probably help with that, but replacing management with measurement is nothing short of measure-mental.

I have updated the PowerPoint slides that I use when discussing metrics:

People manage to the measures!
Sometimes they even manipulate the measures!

A metrics scorecard acts like a car's dashboard.
If you watch it instead of the road, you will crash!

4

Standardized Human Asset Management Is a SHAM

How Performance Management Demoralizes the Performers

▷ **Performance management systems only enforce the strategic objective of implementing performance management systems**

While the '80s and '90s saw the rise of strategy and process consulting, the new millennium brought with it a focus on human asset management. The last piece of the command-and-control structure of the strategy, processes, and metrics framework is the people required to enact it. Although "human asset management" and "human capital management" were the original names given to the practice of managing a company's people, they have largely been replaced with "talent management" due to the industrial connotations of human assets. Some people don't react well to being labeled similarly to a line item on a balance sheet. However, the legacy of that term is the ubiquitous corporate declaration of "People are our greatest asset!" which you'll find on every company website and in every annual report.

Human asset management systems include a slate of human resources processes and methods, including performance management, incentive compensation, competency development, career planning, leadership development, career and leadership coaching, succession planning, and learning management. In this chapter, I will cover only performance management and incentive compensation, and I will discuss other aspects of HAM in the next three. (I couldn't resist the SHAM title.)

Even though the fields of strategy development and process reengineering consulting are crowded, I am often overwhelmed by the multitudes of consulting, coaching, and software companies offering solutions for all your talent management needs. I hate the copy on these companies' websites and in talent management promotional materials because it has such a dire tone urging use of these systems. Much of this tone can be traced back to the book *The War for Talent* published in 2001 by three McKinsey consultants who coined the term "the talent war." The book was written during the dot-com bubble with the premise that because aging baby boomers would leave the workplace faster than young people could enter it, companies would have a talent crisis in the upcoming decades wherein they would not be able to fill vital leadership roles. Of course, the authors didn't predict the economic crisis of 2008 wherein young people wouldn't be able to enter the workforce at all. (I'm trying really, really hard not to say "You can't predict the future!" Oh, darn.)

However, despite the high unemployment rate, the tone of crisis still exists, and without this set of methods and practices in place, a company will be unable to identify and groom future leaders, will lose all its best people to competitors, and will eventually shrivel up and die. It reminds me of the tone of many parenting magazines that play on mothers' fears—if you don't follow the recommended practice, your baby will be in danger. You don't want to put your company in danger, do you? I think the reason the written material has such emotional urgency is because rationally, many of these methods make no sense.

Of the whole alphabet soup of management methodologies, from competitive strategy to competency development, if I had to choose just one that has done the most damage to companies and their employees' lives, the modern performance manage-ment system is the winner. In its current state this system is an automated tool that cascades goals and measures into an em-ployee appraisal and that results in an overall employee rating tied to incentive compensation. With the input of various em-ployee parameters and the click of a few links, an employee's his-tory can be boiled down to a few numbers and her future career with the company ordained. I can't really trace the origins of this system to a book or a method. It seems to have evolved from the management-by-objectives movement that tied compensation to goal achievement. Then someone added competencies and devel-opment planning, and the whole thing got automated.

My first exposure to management by objectives was in the early '90s when I was consulting on a business transformation project that involved both strategy and process work. Although we were already accustomed to creating strategic objectives with targets and breaking those down into individual performance met-rics, this was the first project in which we would tie these specifi-cally into compensation, which we called "pay-for-performance." (I apologize for all the jargon, but this particular field is rife with jargon.) This was also the first time we would base all our work on the balanced scorecard. Fortunately for the company, the soft-ware to do this automatically had yet to be developed, so this particular system was paper based and applied only to the top levels of management.

When the HR consulting team explained how they were creating a compensation system based on target achievement, I was captivated. The compensation piece was what was missing from my other projects, and this was the linchpin that ensured the whole organization did as it was supposed to do. This way, clients had to implement our recommendations; otherwise, they wouldn't get their bonuses. It was perfect! Plus, it was great for consulting firms. Strategy consultants could bring in their other arm, operations consultants, to develop the metrics, the targets, and the collection and reporting processes while HR consulting teams could design the compensation systems, goal development, and performance evaluation processes. Then the IT consultants could automate the whole thing. Over the next decade, I observed the growth of performance management systems from big players like PeopleSoft and SAP to specialized companies like Success Factors and Halogen and the consulting firms that could help implement them. Everyone I know who works in a large company is subject to some version of a performance management system.

In 2000, I left consulting and joined a division of a Fortune 100 company that was acquired by another in 2007. I got to experience firsthand all the havoc we consultants had been wreaking for years with this system. Performance management at both places was an automated process that consumed the last six weeks of every year. This is work that does not contribute to developing new products or services or helping customers. Yet every year, I spent a good part of November and all of December writing up lengthy reviews, reviewing and approving others' reviews, attending several daylong meetings to haggle over employee ratings, ranking them, identifying high performers, and then having to inform direct reports of their ultimate rating—the number spit out by the system based on their weighted goal achievement, their mastery of leadership competencies, and a comparison with their peers. What started out as a way to implement strategy turned into a system that rates, labels, and tracks employees the same as if they were inventory. No wonder it was called "human asset management." It is!

An elegant methodology that theoretically would eliminate nonstrategic work and ensure an aligned and motivated workforce ended up in practice to have the opposite effect. This model is a sham in so many ways that it's difficult to know where to start enumerating its flaws. Even if we pretend that the assumptions upon which it is based are true—people are motivated only by money, employees improve their performance after being judged and graded by a superior, the whole system is fair and objective, and no one games it for his benefit—the sheer amount of effort, time, and costs involved in implementing, administering, and maintaining such a system is enough of an argument against it.

Let's start with what's involved in implementing this type of compensation system, assuming that it's done with every effort to be fair across the company. Typically, the first step is to determine the salary increases, bonuses, stock options, and stock grants by job and performance level. (Or better yet, the first step is to hire a consulting firm to do this for you.) For instance, under a new reward system, a manager performing at a satisfactory level would get a certain percentage of bonus and salary increase and, perhaps, a package of stock or stock options. That sounds easy enough, but it assumes that the company has standard job levels across all functions. In my experience, a manager in one department is very different from a manager in another and even more so if the company has more than one line of business. If the company has grown as the result of mergers or acquisitions—and seriously, what company hasn't—then job levels are probably really inconsistent.

The company therefore needs to implement standard job levels company-wide or at least group the current levels into a set of standards. This is the only way to ensure fairness. Anyone who has experienced standardizing titles and job levels knows that this is a highly emotionally charged and political process. Slotting every employee into a level is a huge undertaking, and its aftermath is a vast swath of disgruntled employees. A senior manager doesn't enjoy being demoted to a manager (it rarely goes the other way), nor does an associate director like finding out her job level is the same as a senior manager's. All those years of clawing your way up that extra rung of the corporate ladder vanish with a stroke of the delete button.

The next step is to standardize the performance appraisal forms and ratings. Again, if the company has silos or has grown through acquisitions, a variety of forms and scales are likely in use. Some departments will want a 1 to 10 scale while others will want 1 to 5. It takes another company-wide effort to agree on one system and method, but with some cajoling and compromise, this can be done in a couple of months.

The third step is to develop a simple process governing when goals need to be written, how goals will trickle down from the corporate goals, when appraisals need to be completed, and when rewards will be distributed. And the last step is to communicate the new process, calendar, and form to all employees and offer training if needed.

However, after a paper-based system is implemented, a few wrinkles appear:

• Not all goals are created equal. Some people have a knack for writing easily achievable goals. Other goals can't be readily quantified or measured for achievement. Plus, managers' expectations of their direct reports vary widely. A standard method of writing goals is needed.

• Performance is very subjective. What one person judges as "meets expectations," another person judges as "exceeds expectations." This also calls for some standardization.

• Developing goals at the beginning of the year to be rated on at the end does not allow enough flexibility to respond to changing business conditions. People need the ability to change goals during the year, but changes would have to be subject to approval or else people would constantly update their goals to what they have already done, defeating the whole purpose of setting goals.

• Waiting until the end of the year to review goals does not give anyone the opportunity to course-correct if goals are not being met. Managers and employees will need to review goals more than once a year.

• A tremendous amount of paperwork is involved that needs to be managed!

At this point, most companies realize that they can't manage this process with paper. Today, tons of software packages are available, so it's likely that this process will be automated. This does require a whole new project, however, to both implement an IT system and to address the deficiencies above, which means several new initiatives are needed:

• Development or purchase of an information system. (Cue the information technology consultants.)

• Creation of the infrastructure needed for the system, including the hardware and the staff for development, maintenance, and user training and support.

• Company-wide training and communications on how to write SMART goals.

• Manager training on how to rate performance objectives fairly.

• Business processes to ensure fair assessment across departments, like cross-functional calibration meetings.

• HR command-and-control functions to ensure fairness of goals and ratings and the accuracy of information.

• Periodic reviews to update goals and course-correct and documentation regarding these periodic reviews.

What is the result? An organization that spends a significant amount of time writing goals, reviewing goals, revising goals, ensuring SMART compliance, approving revised goals, summarizing performance to date, reviewing performance with managers, attending calibration sessions to compare ratings and force-rank employees into a normal distribution curve (which results in another revision of goals and ratings), and approving periodic reviews in an information system. And let's not forget about updating and maintaining the performance review system and, of course, learning how to use the information system and how to comply with all the steps involved. Basically, most of the last quarter of the year is devoted to this process. If the reviews are done semiannually, add two weeks in the summer, too. In addition to losing weeks of work to this rating process, the company has added overhead in the form of HR and IT personnel needed to manage the system, staff a help desk, and collate reports as well as the ongoing costs of hardware and software. Worst of all, managers have less time to spend with their direct reports because of all the requisite paperwork and mandatory meetings.

Remember the point of the pay-for-performance system? It was to focus everyone on the corporate goals to ensure the entire organization was carrying out the strategy. Instead, we have a huge administrative burden that doesn't actually contribute to executing the strategy, unless your strategy is managing goals and implementing incentive compensation. This wouldn't be so bad if it actually helped improve employee motivation and morale and, hence, performance, but in my experience, it does the opposite. The reality is that such systems are designed to dole out money, not to provide feedback to employees or help managers coach their direct reports. Instead, they take time away from relationships and impose a set of standards into which one is required to fit people.

Let's review the assumptions upon which these systems are based:

1. These systems are fair and objective.
2. Being evaluated and graded by a superior improves performance.
3. People are motivated by money.
4. People won't game the system (covered in the previous chapter).

▷ No amount of effort will ensure fairness in a process that is inherently unfair

These systems don't even come close to being fair and objective. At most, they just pretend to by using numbers, checklists, and formulas. The use of SMART goals is supposed to be a best practice to ensure objectivity and fairness. However, in the last chapter, I showed how numerical targets contribute to game playing, working at cross-purposes, and limiting judgment. The other reality is that not every job responsibility lends itself to the SMART format. In fact, many jobs themselves are ill defined and depend on responsiveness to customer demands, competitor actions, or other changes in the environment. Many companies cite "being responsive to customer and changing marketplace needs" as an important value, but how do you predict and measure these responses to add them to your goals?

Here's an example of a problem I once had. One of my direct reports was responsible for responding to employees' calls for help with computer problems. To rate her performance, I was planning to ask some of the people she helped for feedback. However, the HR team insisted that the goal be written in the SMART standard. They suggested I add "helping x number of employees in a month," but I only wanted her to help those who called and not have her solicit calls or be penalized if fewer people called. Then they suggested that we implement a customer satisfaction index by surveying everyone who called. Everyone who called for help would now be burdened with filling out a survey, thus annoying people and inhibiting calls. (Don't you hate those customer service surveys?) Not to mention, tallying the survey results would be a new job responsibility for her and would have to be added to her goals. This particular goal caused so much consternation with HR that I had to make it a minor part of my employee's official rating even though it was a big part of her job, which, when you think about it, really wasn't fair to her.

The other problem with SMART goals is that they cannot address the differences in managers' expectations of their employees. Some people just naturally expect more from their direct reports and others, less. For example, one year, my colleagues and I were discussing why one woman was receiving the highest rating allowed. She was a low-level financial analyst who had recently been promoted from an administrative assistant position after obtaining her bachelor's degree. Formerly my AA, she and I were still friendly. She often complained to me that her boss treated her as if she were incompetent. Even though she had been an AA, she had worked in finance for almost twenty years and had picked up a lot of knowledge. Yet her manager treated her as if she had no relevant experience. Due to her colleagues' absences from a confluence of maternity leave, jury duty, and illnesses, she was the only one in her group during a quarter closing, which she completed unassisted. For her, it was a lot of work but no big deal. She had been doing as much for years, yet her manager was blown away. Her written goals consisted mainly of basic data entry and administrative tasks. She had far exceeded the expectations, which had been way too low. In her manager's eyes, she should have been ecstatic with her rating. However, she felt insulted by the process. An employee was demotivated by receiving the highest possible rating on a performance appraisal!

That year, I had someone at the same level as the financial analyst accomplishing much more complex work who ended up receiving a lower rating to accommodate this situation in the forced ranking of employees. Again, this wasn't fair. Even though everyone was working with SMART goals, lots of unfairness and subjectivity were going on.

These issues are not exceptional, but represent what typically happens during these ranking sessions. The intent of these meetings is to objectively compare goals and ratings, impartially align them, and systematically slot people into the normal distribution curve. But how can we be detached and objective if we are personally invested in the success of our employees? How can we be good managers if we are not personally invested in the success of our employees? Instead of unemotionally cranking out ratings, we sit there endlessly wrangling, arguing over tenths and hundredths of a percentile to give one employee an edge over another. When we calculate the compensation impact of what we are arguing about, and it's about $10 a month, we wonder why we are debating. The debate is not about the money. It's about that number. My employees are inherently better than yours simply because they are mine, and it's my duty to fight for the best number possible. Far from being fair and impartial, these are the most emotional and biased meetings I have ever attended. Unfortunately, the most eloquent managers with the most passionate arguments win. I pity the employees of managers with poor debating skills.

Probably the most biased part of this process is the evaluation meeting, also called the "performance appraisal." Although we like to think that the actual review is objective, because we use SMART goals and lists of competencies, research in the field shows that the evaluation is subject to multiple biases. Among some of the documented biases are these:

- *Favoritism*—We give higher ratings to the people we like.

- *Shared values and social styles*—We like people who are like us so we give them better ratings.

- *Age, race, and sex discrimination*—Again, we give higher ratings to people who are like us or according to perceived stereotypes.

- *Halo/horn effects*—Good or bad performance in one area carries over to our perception of performance in unrelated areas, for example, someone who looks disheveled is perceived to be a poor public speaker and rated accordingly.

- *Our own treatment*—We use the rating *we* receive as the baseline for the ratings we give others.

I can speak to the shared values bias from my career. After a reorganization, I took over a position formerly held by a perfectionist. Perfectionism is at odds with my own philosophy of accomplishing a great many things to about 80 percent satisfaction. My view is that the world changes too fast to try to be perfect. One of my new subordinates, also a perfectionist, who had become accustomed to being praised for her attention to detail, suddenly found herself being coached for improvement! Her less-detailed colleagues, on the other hand, were now better performers than when under their previous boss. No one's performance had actually changed. It was being judged from a different set of criteria, one that wasn't on the appraisal form but was in my head. The performance appraisal process is not fair nor objective in any way, shape, or form. How can it be? It's an evaluation or judgment, the very definition of "subjective."

▷ Let me tell you what I like and don't like about you

Before companies had automated performance management and reward systems, the purpose of performance management was to improve employee performance and provide a baseline to compare employees. We still had performance appraisals, but these didn't have scores and weren't tied directly to rewards. Your manager was given a lot of leeway in determining your salary increases and your overall appraisal. If you had a good manager, you reviewed what went well and what could be improved. In a really good manager-employee relationship, the meeting was a true dialogue where you both reflected on what went well and what didn't, as well as how you could work together better. If you had a poor manager, he used the session to point out all your flaws. (I always figured that this was what was done to him, so he was going to do it to you.)

There is something unnatural about being evaluated by someone else. We don't meet with others to judge their competence in any of our other relationships. I've been married for over twenty years with no annual performance appraisal. I tried it once with my teenage sons, but that didn't work out so well. The problem is that appraisal meetings smack of paternalism. They are based on the assumption that the manager has superior judgment and knows better than the employee what is good for her. The employee's self-appraisal doesn't count in the final assessment.

Now that we have a number on the bottom line of the appraisal, the nature of the conversation can't be anything but a paternalistic evaluation of another being's worth. Because of the SMART goals, listed competencies, and weighted averages, the appraisal appears to be objective, but it can't ever actually be anything but a highly subjective process. It's a game of pretend, a real sham, the worst part of which is that the number prohibits any kind of meaningful dialogue between the manager and employee. The numerical rating is the first thing an employee wants to hear and barely hears anything before that. A real dialogue on how to work better together is replaced by anticipation of the grade.

Regrettably, most employees will be unhappy with what they hear. Because the system forces people into a bell curve to identify high and low performers, the majority of employees will be ranked as average. This conflicts with how we rate ourselves. We all think we are above average. This is a well-documented cognitive bias that has many names: "the better-than-average effect," "illusory superiority," "superiority bias," and even "the Lake Wobegon effect" where all the children are above average. According to Tom Coens and Mary Jenkins in their book *Abolishing Performance Appraisals*, "Virtually all employees see themselves as excellent workers. Most people are disappointed with their ratings and rankings unless they are at the highest level. In fact, studies show that some 98% of workers rate themselves in the top half of performers while 80% rate themselves in the top quarter."

No one likes being told that he is average, especially good performers. To compound this issue, even above-average ratings aren't high enough for the best performers. When I had an appraisal meeting with one of my top performers and informed her of her 4.15 out of 5 rating, an astronomically good rating at this company, which forced most people to a 3, she wanted to know why she wasn't a 5 out of 5. She wanted to know what she did wrong. Instead of having a conversation around what went well, what could have gone better, and what we should do differently, I was stuck explaining the number and trying to convince her that a 4.15 was a really good number and that no one actually got a 5 out of 5. She stewed for days afterward. Again, here was someone demotivated by a really good rating!

I have seen many happy, motivated employees become demoralized by this process. Our underlying assumption number two is wrong: performance is not improved through the appraisal process—rather, just the opposite occurs. The appraisal process deflates people. Performance improves by the coaching and feedback that occur in the daily interactions of people. The communication that occurs between the manager and employee (and with peers) is the vehicle for improving performance. Our current performance management systems are all about filling out forms, calculating scores, doing rankings, and allotting dollars—at the detriment of relationships. Many managers are lulled into thinking that if you follow the process and provide an assessment of strengths and weaknesses with an action plan, then you've got good management covered. Add a few comments about what your direct reports could do better, and, bingo, your job is done until next year. You don't need the relationships because you have the process!

▷ We're not only in it for the money

If you think about it, the ultimate purpose of the entire system is to allot money. The end result is a grade with a dollar amount attached to it. The monetary distribution is the actual final product. It's not a performance management system at all; it's a compensation allotment system. This brings us back to assumption number three—people are motivated by money, that is, tying compensation to goal achievement makes the employee more likely to achieve that goal.

This assumption has been written about a great deal lately. In addition to numerous articles, this topic has accounted for two best-selling books: Alfie Kohn's *Punished by Rewards* and Daniel Pink's more recent *Drive*. *Punished by Rewards* shows how rewards and incentives may have very short-term benefits but in the long-term inhibit learning and intrinsic motivation. Daniel Pink cites studies showing that employees are happiest with a slightly-above-industry-average fixed salary and that the external rewards of bonuses, stock, and so on, have little effect on knowledge workers. Both authors agree that extrinsic reward systems tend to make people less creative and less enthusiastic about their work by destroying their inherent desire to learn, add value to society, and do a job well. By attaching a monetary value to a task, we unwittingly communicate that the task has no value in and of itself. The other effect it has is to limit our thinking. Because we are now so focused on the immediate task, we miss other information that could help us, and we shut down our lateral thinking. In short, the evidence against using incentive compensation as an employee motivator is overwhelming. The only case where it works well is when we want someone to complete a simple, manual task faster, like rewarding factory workers for completing more pieces. However, even that scenario poses a whole set of risks. I've already talked about the harmful consequences of rewarding quantity produced over meeting order commitments. The other consequence is poor quality.

I don't want to rehash all the popular literature on incentives and motivation. You can refer to the bibliography for a few of the studies. I do want to mention the research of a friend of a friend, Marc Hodak, an executive compensation consultant, who in 2006 studied S&P 500 companies and their executive compensation packages and was able to ascertain some best and worst practices. Here are some of his findings:

• Companies that rewarded performance based on balanced scorecard measures underperformed the S&P by 3.5 percent. By focusing on so many measures, executives felt that they were not able to focus on anything.

• Rewarding for a particular measure, like revenue growth, improves that measure but doesn't necessarily translate into profits or shareholder value. Often, individuals will game the system, and meeting the targets for that particular measure will come at the expense of others, like revenue increases at the expense of profit margins.

• People are not motivated by stock options or grants because they perceive that the value of stock is mostly due to economic factors that are out of their control and not due to internal initiatives.

Ultimately, this means that all the effort to align employees around measures and targets and provide money and stock as a motivator has absolutely no proven benefit to a company; rather, it has been proven to have an adverse impact. All that time, money, and effort devoted to standardizing job levels, developing performance criteria and common competencies, agreeing on rating scales and bonus and salary targets, developing forms and processes and automating them, and then filling out forms, conducting calibration meetings, fitting workers into normalized distribution curves, arguing over ratings, attaching dollar distributions to the ratings, and meeting with each employee to discuss the person's strengths and weaknesses and the overall rating and compensation increase has deleterious effects on both worker motivation and a company's performance. So why is this considered a management best practice? Because a few management gurus came up with some interesting models that caught on with management consultants, who thought it seemed like a good idea to meld them together and set about convincing their clients of the supposed benefits without any real knowledge of the consequences. Everything looks so nice and tidy on paper!

Of all the management practices that are unsound and ultimately harmful, this one needs to be eliminated as quickly as possible. In its place, companies should consider a number of alternatives because there really isn't one best way to manage employee performance. When it comes to compensation, my opinion is to go with Daniel Pink's recommendation of an above-average salary and a very simple profit-sharing plan. Offer the same percent reward to everyone when the company meets a profitability threshold. This creates a "we're all in it together" mentality. Stock options and grants are meaningless as part of an expected compensation package but can be used as rewards after the fact for a job well done. This means you can throw all the weighted goal calculations and calibration ranking sessions out the window and just offer a fixed percentage of profits to everyone when the company succeeds. An added benefit is that all the gaming of the system gets thrown away. This method is inherently fair because everyone gets the same amount. SMART goals and normal distribution curves become irrelevant. Everyone can be above average.

When you get rid of the ratings and evaluations, managers and their employees are free to find the best way to improve their performance together. Without the formal system, managers and employees can decide how often, if ever, they want to meet. I like one-on-one sit-down meetings every other month. Sometimes this reflection is better accomplished with a team to discuss team performance or as part of a project postmortem review. Some manager/employee ratios don't allow the supervisor to really know the employees, let alone provide coaching. In those cases, peer feedback may be a better way. Now that we've freed up almost two months, we have time to conduct all sorts of meaningful review and feedback processes like meeting debriefs, lessons learned after major milestones, and team development sessions. Because these can be done throughout the course of business, and not bottled up and saved for the end of the year, they are more accurate, more timely, and more likely to be enacted.

Employees can write their own goals and make them as challenging as they want without getting penalized. In fact, Peter Drucker, who first came up with the concept of managing by objectives, believed that it was critical for people to develop their own goals. People are much more motivated to work on objectives they created themselves than objectives that were handed down to them. I know I prefer working on the projects I want to work on rather than working on the projects you want me to work on. Plus, goals can change to meet changing market conditions without impacting the system. Of course, the managers and the employees would be responsible for ensuring the goals are aligned with the corporate goals, but if you can't trust your managers and employees to work toward corporate goals, then you have a bigger problem than goal alignment.

The only way to address individual performance is individually. This means the one-size-fits-all approach with standardized forms, meeting agendas, checklists, and formulas works only for the standardized employee. I have yet to meet one. Together, management and staff can figure out how to work together better to achieve the company's goals. Isn't that a much better use of everyone's time than rating, ranking, sorting, and labeling employees like some kind of inventoried human asset?

5

I Am a Manager, and So Can You

Why Is the Successful Manager's Handbook 609 Pages Long?

▷ **There's no shortage of management models and techniques**

At various times during my consulting career, I've found myself providing management training. The demand for management skills training seems to be perennially high. Having a bad manager or a bad relationship with a manager is among the most frequent reasons why people leave companies, so good management is a vital concern for businesses. Plus, improving employee performance is one of a manager's main responsibilities, and that is not an easy thing to do. Fortunately, there are lots of consultants in this business and, with them, lots of management theories and models. I still have a handy-dandy envelope of quick reference cards that I helped develop at Gemini years ago that show a variety of models:

- Coaching for behavior change (five steps)
- Giving effective feedback (seven components)
- Receiving feedback as a gift (six steps)
- PACR (paraphrase, ask, check, respond) listening technique

- AIR (acknowledge, investigate, reinforce) model for dealing with resistance
- Trust formula
- Partners chart
- Stages of team development
- Plus, many more (thirty-six in total)

Since then, I have attended four leadership training programs, including not one but two women's leadership programs, and have become acquainted with many more management models. So what exactly is good management technique? What's more important—coaching and feedback or delegating work or developing employees? To answer the age-old question of good management, I started pulling out all the relevant materials from my bookshelves. For my purposes in this chapter, I am going to use the terms "leadership" and "management" synonymously, fully aware that some leadership gurus (or is that management gurus?) have made a career of differentiating the two. Personally, I've never been able to comprehend how you can be a great leader without being a great manager. How do you get to a position of leadership without succeeding as a manager? How can you be a great manager without knowing how to inspire and motivate people?

Anyway, I pulled out some of the books from these umpteen programs, and the first one that caught my eye was the *Successful Manager's Handbook*. I'm not sure where or when I got this, but it is used as the textbook for Southwest Airlines' leadership program. It is 609 pages long, excluding the index and appendices, and was written by a team of consultants at Personnel Decisions International, a large and imposing human resources consultancy. PDI is responsible for a number of trademarked models and assessments; perhaps its PROFILOR 360-degree feedback tool is the most famous. The *Successful Manager's Handbook* is built around the PDI Leadership Success Wheel, which is divided into four categories of capabilities:

- Self-leadership
- Results leadership
- People leadership
- Thought leadership

These four leadership areas are broken down into nine factors total (e.g., a communications factor and a strategy factor), which are composed of thirty-two skills. "Inspire trust," "champion change and innovation," "think strategically," and "drive for results" are some of the skills needed to master leadership success. These skills are broken down further into more detailed tasks or attributes. For instance, "champion change and innovation" has three components—"develop personal creativity," "encourage innovation in others," and "champion change initiatives." Each of these components has its own set of parts. These skills probably sound familiar because they form the template for many of the leadership competency models used in companies today. Altogether, I counted 433 separate attributes or actions that comprise successful leadership ability. Each of these has a chapter explaining how to accomplish it, hence the 609 pages. The chapters describe the skills and offer tips, how-tos, extensive step-by-step instructions, templates, information on more resources, and even some relevant cartoons. While some of the tips border on the inane, "readily put in extra effort to accomplish important tasks," the book does give an overview of many business planning tools that may be unfamiliar to a new manager. To be honest, I never used this book. In case you didn't pick up on it, this book is 609 pages long! Every time I open this book I get a headache. I know that it is meant as a reference book, but I find it impossible to even assimilate the table of contents so I know when to refer to it.

Next to it on the shelf, in stark contrast, is *Leadership and the One Minute Manager*. This slim volume of 107 pages (large print on small pages), was written by another HR consulting powerhouse, Ken Blanchard. This book explains the Situational Leadership model using an apocryphal tale of an entrepreneur looking for advice from a well-known manager. Years ago when I took a Situational Leadership training class, I received this book along with a stack of other material stamped with the model—a wall poster, a wallet card, a white paper, several CDs with e-learning modules, and a cardboard contraption that I can't readily identify the purpose of. The Situational Leadership model, perhaps the most popular management model and certainly the best branded, is based on a theory jointly developed by Ken Blanchard and Paul Hersey. They went their separate ways, resulting in each creating his own version of the Situational Leadership model.

Blanchard's version of the model (SLII) says that there are four types of management styles: directing, coaching, supporting, and delegating. There are also four development levels of employees determined by their levels of competence and commitment. The main point of the model is that the management or leadership style you use is situational, depending on the ability and experience of the employee. If the employee has a new task, you would use the directing style and basically tell the employee what to do, providing close supervision. If the employee is familiar with but not competent in the task and is experiencing some doubts or confidence issues, you would use the coaching style and provide encouraging feedback as well as specific instructions. The supporting style lets the employee make decisions and complete the task with the manager facilitating the process and providing support along the way. The delegating style lets the employee do the task on her own. You use the model by meeting with your employee and explaining the different styles. Together you decide which management technique is most appropriate for the situation. The model also states that the leader must ensure the goals of the task are clear, observe the performance, and provide feedback. Hersey's version of the model is similar, but he uses the terms "telling, selling, participating, and delegating." Because he's not the marketing powerhouse that the Ken Blanchard Companies are, when you hear the term "Situational Leadership," it probably refers to the SLII model.

In contrast, a leadership model developed by Robert Tannenbaum and Warren H. Schmidt in 1958 and published in "How to Choose a Leadership Pattern" advocates for choosing one leadership style to avoid confusion and mismatched expectations among subordinates. This model describes a continuum of management styles ranging from autocratic on one end to laissez-faire on the other end. In the middle are styles that can be described as persuasive, participative, facilitating, or democratic. Choosing a style depends on the culture of the company, the abilities and expectations of the direct reports, and the ability and confidence of the manager. If the gap between the capabilities of the manager and the direct reports is big, an autocratic style is appropriate. If the gap is small, a laissez-faire style is better. The success of a manager is due to an understanding of his own values and capabilities, an understanding of the needs and desires of his subordinates and the necessities of the particular situation, and the manager's ability to act accordingly.

If you prefer more recent work, Daniel Goleman, who developed the concept of emotional intelligence, also developed a leadership model. His model is based on the concept of resonance, which is the ability to tap into other people's feelings and move them in a positive direction. People with high emotional intelligence are able to resonate with others. Goleman believes that the emotions of the leader affect the emotions of the employees and identifies six leadership styles that can resonate—visionary, coaching, affiliative, democratic, pacesetting, and commanding. All the styles are appropriate in certain circumstances; however, the latter two styles are more autocratic and can have a negative impact on an organization if overused.

Are you tired of leadership models yet? I am, though I've barely scratched the surface. My point is to give you the context that there are a lot of models and theories out there and that this stuff is taken very seriously. Given this context, in March 2011, Google released the results of a two-year study called "Project Oxygen" to determine what traits make a good manager. Google decided to do its own research and analyzed thousands of performance appraisals and feedback surveys to arrive at its own model. Its findings made headlines in the business section of the *New York Times* as well as receiving countless mentions in business and technology blogs. Here, in order of importance, are the findings of Google's groundbreaking study:

Google's Eight Habits of Highly Effective Managers
1. Be a good coach.
2. Empower your team and don't micromanage.
3. Express interest in employees' success and well-being.
4. Be productive and results-oriented.
5. Be a good communicator and listen to your team.
6. Help your employees with career development.
7. Have a clear vision and strategy for the team.
8. Have key technical skills so you can help advise the team.

This new model received both lots of derision and lots of praise in the press. These golden rules have been the basis of management fundamentals for at least fifty years. Anyone who has read basic management books or attended management training could tell you this. However, this model is pretty simple

compared with others, and its principles are ordered by importance and backed by data!

▷ How I inadvertently managed to manage

The fact that Google, one of the world's most admired and imitated companies, felt the need to conduct a study of what makes a
manager good underscores what a conundrum good management
is in the business world. Everyone recognizes its importance,
many companies have mandated manager training programs, yet
few companies can say that they have excellent managers. It's a
Sisyphean task. It doesn't matter how much time, money, and
attention is devoted to good management, no one seems to have
achieved it. Even a company like Pfizer, which uses the Situational
Leadership model and requires managers to attend two weeks of
training, doesn't seem to have cracked this nut. When I was a
manager there, I found myself discussing one of my direct reports
with a vice president in my group. He commented on how this
person's work had surpassed everyone's expectations and how in
general, my team performed really well. He then asked if I could
share my management techniques with the rest of the group.

At first I was pleased with the recognition implicit in this request, but once I thought about it, I was completely taken aback.
I didn't have any management techniques! What was I going to
share? At first I felt like a fraud, but then I had a moment of
revelation. I liked the people who worked for me, and I wanted
to see them succeed. I had good relationships with them. I am
still friends with many of my former bosses and subordinates. I
care about them, they care about me, and on the job, we worked
together to succeed and achieve results. We did this by talking
and being honest. In short, we develop good relationships.

During my career, I've helped turn some poor performers
into top performers. I'd love to pat myself on the back for an

extraordinary talent, but I succeed at this because I like to do it and I put in the effort required. Usually, other managers look at me aghast when we have a problem employee and I offer to take that person in my group. This is contrary to one of the basic tenets of good management—you are supposed to fill your team with the top performers. I know this sounds awful, but taking a poor performer under my wing is similar to taking in a rescue dog. When you give a good situation to an employee who has only known a bad situation, he is yours for life. It's extra work at first, but afterward you are rewarded with an extremely loyal, hardworking, and happy employee. Of course, I choose the people I think have the potential, and admittedly, my track record is pretty good but certainly not 100 percent.

The first time I took a problem employee under my wing was on a large consulting engagement. We were in the selling phase, where we did an initial scoping of the problems and put together a proposal to sell a project. We had a new hire, Frank, who had never consulted before. This project was unusually chaotic, with a very large project team and limited access to the client. Most of us were working from our hotel rooms, but we did have a designated conference room that we used for PCs and printers and checking in with the project manager. A few of us, including Frank, were assigned to review the client's financial reports and benchmark various financial measures with their competitors'. We headed off to the nearest library to use its databases and divvied up the reports among ourselves. The plan was to reconvene the next day to collate our findings and to report those to the project leader the day after. We convened as planned to discuss our findings, but Frank was missing. We left voice mails and called his room, but he didn't answer. During the evening, while we were preparing our findings for the project leader meeting, Frank rushed in excitedly to the conference room. He apologized profusely for missing our meeting. He had returned to the library to investigate some information and lost track of time. He had found some very interesting data and had been working on it all day. We told him we were working on the presentation and would help him present his findings, but he begged off. He had everything in a spreadsheet all ready to go. Although we told him that the expectation was to put our findings in PowerPoint, he was really excited about his material and was confident that the project leader would be sufficiently impressed.

The next day, we presented our findings to the project leader, who naturally had questions and asked us to investigate some findings further. Then it was Frank's turn. He distributed printouts from his spreadsheets, basically rows and rows of data, and began talking animatedly about each number, his eyes glued to the spreadsheet. After about three minutes of details on financial numbers, the project leader shouted, "Stop." Still enthusiastic, Frank asked, "Do you have a question?" "Yes," was the reply, "What the hell is this?" It was not normal to use four-letter words in the course of business, and the whole room burst out laughing. When we all settled down, the project leader shook his head and asked for the next presenter. Frank was crestfallen and humiliated. He also seemed a bit bewildered, and I felt bad for him.

Later that day, I asked Frank to join us for dinner, and he started to decline the invitation. He wanted to do more work on his spreadsheet and redeem himself. I told him rather firmly that it would be a better idea if he joined us. He got the message, and at dinner that night, I learned that this was both his first consulting engagement and his first business experience. He had been in the ROTC program and had a few years in the military but no business or consulting experience. He had excelled as a student and then as an officer and was certain that he would excel as a consultant. His failure earlier in the day was a huge shock to his self-esteem, and he was determined to make amends. I mentioned that his mistake was missing our meeting, where we consolidated our findings and put together the presentation. We knew what was expected, while he obviously didn't. After dinner, we all agreed that we would do our additional research in the morning individually and meet in the afternoon to rework our presentation. This time Frank showed up, and it turned out his finding was something we already had, but we added his supporting evidence to the presentation to make a stronger case. He was disappointed that he hadn't found an amazing revelation, but he had a section to present. In a flash of insight, I asked him to rehearse his section, and he started to delve into the details of his numbers. After a few tries, we worked out exactly what he would say.

Our final presentation went well, the project leader presented it to the client later in the day, and we sold a sizeable piece of work. The next week, the project leader held a meeting where he assigned team leads to different portions of the work. The team leads then started divvying up the consulting resources. When Frank's name came up, the project leader shook his head in consternation. All eyes were suddenly on me. Would I take him on my team? I was pretty new to managing other people, this would be only my second time leading a team, and Frank was going to need a lot of management. However, he was very eager to succeed, worked hard, and responded well to coaching. Plus, I knew that I really didn't have a choice, so I agreed to take him.

Over the next few weeks, I met with my team, and we put together outlines for the client deliverables. After each team meeting, I met separately with Frank and reviewed what I needed from him. On several occasions, he put together something different from what I expected, so I learned to communicate more clearly and also urged him to ask me for clarification whenever he had any doubts. I often drafted what I thought his final product should look like. With a lot of direction, Frank started to get the hang of the engagement. In his favor, he did have an infectious enthusiasm and great people skills. However, every time I had him present his work, he got absorbed in some detail he found fascinating and diverted from the agenda. Because he was well-liked, the client was able to forgive this transgression at our informal meetings, but Frank was not allowed to present his work at the formal client progress meetings. This is a big issue for a consultant and potentially a career ender. Although I coached him repeatedly to stick to the agenda and to summarize, he continued to delve into details. He saw the need to change but just couldn't help himself. He was fascinated by the details and thought we should be, too.

Exasperated, I realized that my coaching was ineffective, and I needed to do something different. I arranged for some of the client's senior management to attend our informal team presentation and explained that their role was to complain vehemently whenever Frank went off track or got too detailed. Frank was unaware that I was setting him up. Surprised at the senior-level attendees at our meeting, he got up to present. After a few minutes, he got lost in the minutiae and received some feedback from his audience. He refocused, excelled for a while, and then got sidetracked again. He received some stronger feedback. After he strayed the third time, the comments got loud and derisive (the client was having fun with this). His audience had become hostile. He was shocked, but suddenly he became aware that he was boring everyone and wasting important people's time. He may have found the details interesting, but we clearly didn't. And we mattered more than he did. I saw the glimmer of realization on his face. He turned to us and said, "I get it. You don't think this is interesting and really don't care. You probably just want to know the highlights."

After that incident, he was a completely different consultant. He stayed focused on the task at hand, and he tailored his work to what others wanted, not what he wanted. He also became my go-to person. He volunteered for everything and overperformed even the smallest tasks. His performance was no longer just about succeeding. It had become very personal. I had shown faith in him, and he was going to make sure he never disappointed me. Although at the beginning of the project, he took a lot of my time and energy, by the end of the project, he was doing the work of two people.

The culmination of the project was a big client presentation where we reviewed all our accomplishments. This was an extremely important presentation because part of our fees were based on realized cost savings. Therefore, the client would have to agree with our results. Frank had fifteen minutes on the agenda to present his work. Many of the consultants who knew Frank only from the beginning of the project asked me to reconsider his involvement. Fortunately, two of the clients who partook in my learning experiment were also at the final presentation, and they expressed their support for Frank. Interestingly, clients usually look to poke holes in consulting presentations and make us dance, but these two were really vested in Frank's success. When his turn came, Frank was a little apprehensive, knowing what the other consultants thought of him, but I had told him to look at me and our two friendly clients. Seeing our positive body language, his confidence grew. He was polished and professional and, even better, engaging. His infectious enthusiasm, which had in the past thrown him off track, was now directed at charming his audience. And he succeeded. I had a hard time keeping my eyes dry; I felt so proud.

He wasn't the only one who learned something important. I learned a great deal. People have very different ways of perceiving the world, for one. What is fascinating to one person is extraneous detail to another. Also, sometimes coaching and feedback aren't enough. You may have to show people their problems rather than talk about them. Plus, I learned something about myself. I never considered myself a "people person." I would describe myself as more interested in intellectual matters than emotional ones, but when Frank got up to speak at the final client presentation and did an excellent job, I felt the biggest sense of accomplishment of my career—even more so when Frank went on to be successful in his later projects.

▷ Being a good manager isn't all that different from being a good person

I had my greatest success as a manager before I learned any management models. This was what I learned from managing Frank, and it so happens that these lessons apply to other areas of my life:

1. Show you care. I want my direct reports (and my peers and my family and my friends) to succeed. I really do. I don't understand frenemies. When my employees succeed, I succeed. I feel great. Because I care about my team, I like to get to know them. I want to know about their home lives, their interests, and their dislikes, not so that I can manage them better, but so that I can have better relationships. I get to know people because I want to get to know people, not as a "technique." This is what makes my life interesting—having relationships with interesting people.

2. Communicate. No one knows what is in your head, not your spouse, not your kids, and certainly not your employees. This was an important lesson I learned with Frank. At the beginning, I would communicate clearly and specifically what I expected, and he would give me something different. Then I would review it again, and again he gave me something different. I was exasperated. However, I am an intelligent person and realize that if something isn't working, you must try something else. Even though I thought I was being very clear and specific, obviously I wasn't to him. That's when I had my own "aha" moment. It was not in my

power to make Frank understand me. There was no way I could get inside his mind and change it. However, it was in my power to make *sure* Frank understood me. I could always ask *him* what was in *his* head. I changed my approach. It is one I still use today, and it goes like this: "I just gave you a list of instructions that was probably not as clear as it could have been. What do you think you should be doing?" Aha! Now I know what's in the other person's head, and I can try again!

3. Be flexible/adaptable/responsive. I'm not sure what the right label is for this rule, but this reflects my number one complaint about the universe. Basically, if something is not working, try something different. Do not keep trying the same method over and over and over and expect that one day it will magically work when it has failed every other time. If coaching doesn't work, try coaching again but in a different way. Perhaps obtain feedback from someone else. Talk with the employee about the causes of the behavior. If that doesn't work, try setting up an experience, like I did with Frank. But don't try the same thing repeatedly and expect it to work!

4. Think and plan ahead. This one isn't so much about managing people as it is about managing work and workloads. Map out what needs to be accomplished and by when and share the information with your team. Meet with stakeholders and find out what they need you to do. Develop a final work plan with your team. This sounds very simple, but I know managers who delegate work without getting input from their team and some who keep their employees in the dark about future projects. They don't want them to worry about what's coming. Put all the work out there, let the whole team see what it is so they know what everyone is working on, and so people can volunteer to take on new tasks and share the workload.

Okay. How does my acquired wisdom stack up against Google's research and the research and models of the academics? Without studies, without extensive data mining, without scholarly credentials, how did I fare? I have only four things, so I win the simplicity category.

Let's return to the Google list. I've reordered it to compare it with Stephen Covey's seven habits of highly effective people in table 1.

Table 1 **Google versus Covey**

Google	Stephen Covey
Eight habits of highly effective managers	Seven habits of highly effective people
4. Be productive and results-oriented.	Be proactive.
7. Have a clear vision and strategy for the team.	Begin with the end in mind. Put first things first.
3. Express interest in employees' success and well-being. 1. Be a good coach.	Think win-win.
5. Be a good communicator and listen to your team.	Seek first to understand, then to be understood.
2. Empower your team and don't micromanage.	Synergize (cooperate creatively).
6. Help your employees with career development.	Sharpen the saw (renew).
8. Have key technical skills so you can help advise the team.	

It's not a perfect match, but considering one is about good business management and the other is about success in life, they have a striking similarity. If I reworded the Google list to make it more generic, wouldn't it be pretty close?

Stephen Covey breaks his habits into three categories:

- Private victory/personal effectiveness, kind of like self-mastery
- Public victory or working with other people
- Renewal or taking the time to improve yourself

I like this breakdown because being a good manager really has three parts—being able to accomplish work, being able to manage others, and helping to develop others' skills. So essentially, being a good manager is very similar to being a good person. An essential part of being a good and effective person is being able to have good relationships. Good management is having good relationships with the people who work for you—listening to them, coaching them, and having open and honest communications where it is okay to clarify any misunderstandings and okay to give feedback (Google rules 1, 3, and 5). These are all components of having a good relationship. The funny thing about having a good relationship with your direct reports is that you trust them; therefore, you don't need to micromanage them (Google rule 2). You also tend to care about their future (Google rule 6.)

Let's revisit the Goleman model based on emotional intelligence (visionary, coaching, affiliative, democratic, pacesetting, and commanding). In essence, Goleman is saying that good leaders need to be empathetic and flexible. The Tannenbaum-Schmidt model specifically states that choosing a leadership style is dependent on the manager's own self-awareness, the needs of her subordinates, and the demands of the particular situation. So again, good leaders need to understand themselves and be empathetic and flexible. My point is that these aren't leadership skills or management skills or business skills. These are life skills.

Revisiting the Situational Leadership model, a manager is supposed to choose a style that matches the needs of the subordinates. A manager does this by meeting with his direct reports and discussing their needs and the appropriate leadership styles. Gemini Consulting, years ago, had a practice of conducting an expectations review between the project manager and the consultant at the beginning of a project. During this meeting, you met with your project manager to determine your goals on the project and your expectations for how you would work together. The goals were the "what" of your work, while the expectations were "how" you liked to work. You talked about how you liked to be managed and what kind of support you needed. Your manager talked about what she needed from you regarding information updates and communications. This was when you both figured out how capable and confident you were of doing the job. I found these meetings incredibly useful because the two of you discussed how best to work together. The greatest value of using the Situational Leadership model is having the conversation between the manager and the direct report. The model forces you to communicate, gives you language to communicate with, and forces you to be flexible in your approach.

This is my point: good management technique is not rocket science, people. Why are we overcomplicating this? To be a good manager, first, you have to be able to manage yourself and get things done, and second, you need to be able to have good relationships with those around you. You should also think about the future, yours and your team's, but that's a lower priority. Good management skills are good relationship skills. That's it. End of story. No need to overthink this. It's not a technique or a science at all. It is knowing how to have good relationships.

I've read a couple of management advice books that strongly caution against being friends with your direct reports. The advice is illustrated with an anecdote along these lines: we used to be friends, then I got promoted, and then my friend turned in a piece of work that was garbage and expected me to be okay with it. Or he didn't turn in the work and expected me to cover for him—or to do it myself. My reaction to such stories is, What kind of friendship is that? My friends would never take advantage of me that way. Those aren't friends. Those are enemies.

My own experience is that when you have a boss you love, you do anything for her. You do this because you know that she would do anything for you. I've been lucky to have that kind of relationship both upward and downward. I've often had to beg my team to go home and warn them that they were taking their jobs much too seriously. If I got too involved in their work, they told me nicely to back off, and if they needed help, they came into my office looking for it. This is what people do. This is how people naturally act with other people. The reason some managers don't behave this way is because they've been taught by experts that management is a science or set of rules or a methodology whereby you must act unnaturally and follow guidelines instead of your own judgment.

The world does not need any more management models or methods. The ones we have work just fine, or don't work just fine, because the models are not what have the real value. The conversations with our employees about how to work together are what have value. So does gaining the wisdom that there is more than one right way to work with people. If you are spending your time reading 609 pages of how to manage your people, then you are not actually managing your people. All these devices are just ways to avoid what you really should be doing. The only right way to deal with people is to actually deal with people, not to read about dealing with people, to prepare a checklist on how to deal with people, or to study how to deal with people. The more time we spend figuring out how to deal with people, the less time we spend actually dealing with people. And if I'm at a loss with how to work with you, I can seek advice from all sorts of places and books and classes, but the most effective method is to seek that advice from you.

6

Stop Perpetrating Talent Management on People

Albert Einstein Was *Not* an A Player

▷ **Let's stop sorting out the ABCs**

By now you may have realized that I haven't personally broken any companies, at least not that I know of. But consultants have broken companies, and I would like to talk about the most famous case—Enron. Although the role of Arthur Andersen in helping Enron with some creative accounting was widely reported, another consulting company that was deeply embedded at Enron, McKinsey, managed to escape the scandal relatively unscathed. I mentioned the book *The War for Talent* earlier, but I neglected to mention that one of the reasons this book has fallen out of favor is that it uses Enron as one of its main case examples. Jeffrey Skilling was a former McKinsey employee, and he implemented many of the management principles written about in this book at Enron. (To be fair, the McKinsey consultants faulted Enron because the company didn't implement these principles correctly.)

While most of the recommendations in this book are relatively mild (create a talent mindset, develop and coach employees, be more creative in recruiting), one principle alarms me and is the one that contributed most to Enron's downfall—differentiate your employees and then manage them accordingly. The book recommends sorting out your A, B, and C players and treating them differently. A players (typically, your top 10–20 percent) should get most of the rewards and be given as much latitude as possible to pursue opportunities and advance their careers. A players determine the future of the company and because of their constant need to be challenged, are likely to leave if neglected. C players (your bottom 10–20 percent) should be coached until their performance improves or be let go. While most of the attention should go to As and Cs, B players should be affirmed that they are still worthy and should be developed as needed. This differentiation method is sometimes referred to as the "star system" or "rank and yank," depending on whether you are in the top or the bottom rank. While I doubt that McKinsey was the first company to devise this kind of differentiation, it did create this popular terminology and propagate this philosophy as a best practice.

How this philosophy contributed to Enron's demise was that it created a highly competitive and arrogant environment that encouraged excessive risk taking and cheating, where stars were led to believe that they could do no wrong because they had "talent." If you were a talented A player, you were given considerable leeway without oversight to start new business ventures. Failures were not considered bad, just a sign that you were indeed a risk taker, an affirmation of your A-player status. Malcolm Gladwell, in a *New Yorker* piece about Enron, cites examples of A players given extreme latitude, one of whom was Lou Pai. Pai created Enron's power-trading business, which lost millions of dollars, and then went on to run the electricity-outsourcing business, which lost even more money.

While this philosophy is, of course, unfair and even ruthless, my main problem with it is the assumption that there are definitive A, B, and C players. I am confused by the assumptions upon which the star philosophy is based. In *The War for Talent*, one chapter talks about how a poor performer was discharged from the Naval Academy but was given a second chance with a proactive mentor and then eventually became a great leader. So in this case, a C performer who should have been culled due to a track record of poor performance was given mentoring and became an A performer. Then the very next chapter recommends implementing the A, B, and C player system. So if C players could become B or A players, and B players could become C or A players, couldn't A players become C or B players? Especially with no oversight? Do you mentor C players until they become Bs or keep at it until they become As? If you mentor C players to become As, what about the Bs? Shouldn't it be even easier to make them As? How do you know when a player has reached his final destination?

▷ Performance is situational

Like almost everyone is familiar with the Enron implosion, almost everyone knows something of the life of Albert Einstein. His name and visage are synonymous with genius. He has been described as one of the most important physicists ever. In 1999, *Time* magazine named him the Person of the Century, not Scientist of the Century, but Person. His most famous work is his general theory of relativity, but he actually won his Nobel Prize for the photoelectric effect. In 1905, he wrote four groundbreaking papers on the photoelectric effect, specific relativity, Brownian motion, and the equivalence of mass and energy ($E=mc^2$). Each of these was worthy of the Nobel Prize. He predicted black holes and wormholes. He was the author of over three hundred scientific papers, and the list of important physics theories he conceived is way too long for me to include here.

One of the things that Einstein most regretted is that his father died in 1903, before anyone had heard of Einstein. In his father's eyes, Einstein was a total failure. He left his primary school before graduating—on less-than-spectacular terms. The story of his failing math is apocryphal but is based on one of his teachers' declaration that he would never amount to anything. He failed his first entrance exam to get into the Zurich Polytechnic School. After remedial work, he was admitted to the school, but his unconventional thinking and tendency to skip classes irked his teachers. When he left the polytechnic, none of his teachers recommended him for a job. Stuck with low-level tutoring jobs, he was fired even from those. His personal life was also a mess. A Jew, he wanted to marry a Christian woman against his parents' wishes, and they had a child out of wedlock, whose fate is unknown today. (The couple did marry, but that marriage ended in a very messy and bitter divorce.) Eventually, a friend helped him get a job as a clerk at the Bern patent office. There, he was passed over for promotion, not having enough engineering experience. Bored, he wrote his four convention-shattering scientific papers and changed the world.

If one were to ask Einstein's teachers about his chances of success, you would likely get some head shaking and tsk-tsks. Although his abilities in science and math were evident, he was by all accounts unconventional, free thinking, headstrong, and uncoachable, not the qualities people were looking for in academia at the turn of the century. However, it is exactly these qualities that made him an exceptional theoretical scientist. To boil it down, he would never fit in with the strict pedagogy of schools in the early 1900s and would not be a good teacher in that environment. He probably wouldn't have been good in an engineering job, either, not being known to follow instructions. Ironically, if Einstein had managed to obtain a more prestigious job out of college, he would have been deemed more successful, but he probably wouldn't have had the time to work on his theories. Hence, he never would have obtained the ultimate success and fame he achieved. In many ways, he was lucky he found the position at the patent office.

Another famous individual with a track record of failure is Ulysses S. Grant. Before the Civil War, he failed at running businesses, failed at farming, and failed at real estate. However, contrary to everyone's expectations, he turned out to be a great military commander, even against the renowned Robert E. Lee. Although history books write about the inevitability of the Union's triumph due to its industries, they don't spend much time on how the best military officers of the time sided with the Confederacy. Lincoln had a hell of a time finding someone competent to lead the Union army. Grant's name didn't appear on any short list of potential leaders. Although he had a solid reputation after the Mexican War, his military career afterward wasn't noteworthy. He eventually left the army when it required him to be away from his family for extended periods of time, causing him to drink heavily. He didn't have much of a reputation when he volunteered early in the war to train soldiers. Mostly he was known for drinking, smoking, and losing money. However, he did have three unique capabilities that made him a great general: an uncanny ability to use the lay of the land to his advantage, a knack for supply logistics, and the ability to both instill discipline and inspire his men. He was unpretentious and greatly loved by his troops. Grant's popularity was so great that he was elected president of the United States. Unfortunately, his administration was plagued by scandals and corruption, and his presidency presided over the abuses of the Reconstruction era. He was accused of being more interested in rewarding his army cronies than in rebuilding the country.

Throughout his life, Grant battled problems with alcohol and seemed to be drunk at the least opportune times, like at meetings with superior officers. After his presidency, he was still popular, especially in Europe, and was invited to speak and socialize among high society. It was a good thing that he had well-connected friends because he lost all his money in a family-run investment firm that turned out to be a front for a scam. His friend Mark Twain urged him to write his memoirs, and even though he was dying of throat cancer, Grant worked on his autobiography, driven by the need to provide income for his family after his death. He finished the book on his deathbed, and it became a best seller. In fact, it is still on bookshelves today, well over a hundred years later, and is considered to be one of the best military memoirs ever. So was U. S. Grant an A player, a B player, or a C player?

He was a great general, a good writer, a poor president, and a horrendous businessman, so he was a good performer in some situations and a poor performer in others. This is not unusual. We know from our experiences that people have their strengths and weaknesses. In certain areas, we excel, and in others, not so much. However, if you have management responsibilities in an American corporation, according to this talent management best practice, you are asked to evaluate your employees and put them into the high-, medium-, and low-performing buckets, where they are subsequently labeled as stars or dogs or mediocre players. Employees are tracked according to their performance rankings. Although this designation should be made based on a long history, there are times, like in the case of a new hire or a merger, when managers are required to rank their direct reports after just one review. Where would you rank Einstein in 1903? What about Grant in 1859?

▷ The problem with labels is that labels stick

Speaking as someone who has usually been designated as a top performer—graduating near the top of my class, attending a prestigious school, working for a think tank, working as a management consultant, and then working for Fortune 100 companies—I would like to be honest about my own career performance. I have been in situations where I've failed miserably. The first time I performed poorly was at a manufacturing client where we needed to investigate its costs. Due to an accounting change, product costs skyrocketed, and we were hired to calculate a better way to determine product costs. This was in the '80s, and I was carrying around a "portable" Compaq computer, which was less like a laptop and more like a full-sized air conditioning unit with a handle. I hurt my back hoisting it into the trunk of a rental car. A local doctor prescribed Tylenol with codeine. That's when I learned that I don't react well to codeine. It made me depressed and weepy. Part of the job was to develop a huge spreadsheet to detail all the costs, and details are not my forte. Typical for a consulting engagement, we were working long hours, and I had to sit for long periods of time on an uncomfortable chair in front of a computer. In pain, fatigued, and reacting to the codeine, I kept transposing numbers in the spreadsheet and putting them in the wrong cells. I just could not enter my data correctly. Everyone was infuriated with me because my errors were invalidating everyone else's work. We had to double-check and triple-check everything I touched. Worse, I would cry whenever someone reprimanded me.

When I returned to my home office, I had to sit down with the practice head to discuss my performance issues. Even though

I had other project successes under my belt and was requested by partners from other offices, after that one failure, I was suddenly a problem. The gist of the conversation was that I needed to improve or else I would receive a bad write-up at the year's end. That meant no bonus and no salary increase and probably no future in the company. I was incredulous. I had a solid track record, but none of that mattered. I had been labeled. All it took was one failure. Afterward, I had to find work from the other offices.

Another time when I gave a less-than-stellar performance was when my kids were preschool age and my mother became terminally ill and needed constant care. On top of being ill, she had some big legal issues that I was suddenly responsible for. Between taking care of my kids, caring for my mom, finding the right doctors and treatments, and wrangling with lawyers, my job came in at fifth priority in my life. I think I spent most of my workday on the phone with hospitals, doctors, and lawyers and not too much on my work. Somehow, I managed to turn in an average performance that year. (I wrote easily achievable goals.) I remember talking with my manager, who wondered why I wasn't living up to my potential. Again, I was incredulous. How could all my personal issues not affect my performance?

My worst experience was the engagement I mentioned earlier when I had been assigned to improve the scheduling function but found the problem was with the business model, not the scheduling methods. The whole new consulting team arrived and insisted that I use their methodology, which I believed was inappropriate for the problem at hand. Aside from disagreeing on the approach, when it was clear that we would not be able to come up with the promised cost savings, the project management decided that headcount reductions could account for the rest. The awful task of determining which heads to cut fell to me although I had already assured the client that I wasn't there to recommend layoffs. I refused to name potential layoff candidates, causing even more ire. To make matters worse, I accidentally bad-mouthed the project manager in front of the client, a huge consulting blunder, and that got back to him. From then on, I was labeled not only as incompetent but also as "a loose cannon" and "not a team player." I was told that I had no future in consulting, even though I had been a successful consultant for a number of years.

Even more mysteriously, I suddenly couldn't do anything right. I was asked to put together a presentation, something I normally do well, and it was critiqued as terrible. When I put together a form to use to keep track of changeovers that the project manager liked, the credit for authorship went to another consultant. I had been labeled, and everything I did was seen through that label. My history of performance was irrelevant. On my next project, I was assigned a manager who oversaw and double-checked everything I did. It took a couple of months before he realized that I was neither incompetent nor insubordinate. I was quite capable but had just come from a bad situation.

Isn't that how we naturally describe failure? We don't describe ourselves as failures all the time, just in certain situations. Einstein was in a bad situation when he needed to fit in with the scientific orthodoxy and please his teachers. He was an iconoclast by nature—in most situations, that was his undoing, and in another, his gift to the world. Grant excelled at logistics but stank at managing businesses and, especially, money. He really did not have the right skills or inclinations to be a good president, although he was a brilliant wartime leader. I have strengths and weaknesses, too, and often they are different sides of the same thing. I am great at seeing the whole picture and at getting at the roots of problems. I am not very good at remembering details and following methodologies.

Fortunately, because of my strengths, I have more often been labeled as an A player than a C. This label sticks as well. On a project where I was improving capital investments, I had made the recommendation to hedge investments made in local currencies. This was advice that came from the client's own financial group that I recommended to top management. About a week after this recommendation was implemented, the peso's value dropped by half. The client had made large investments in pesos, and hedging the currency forestalled a potential loss of hundreds of millions of dollars. It was pure luck that I had made the recommendation beforehand. At the time, I knew little about finance and even less about the global economy. Yet I got the credit for making a prescient business recommendation. Afterward, I was treated like a rock star. I was included in all sorts of meetings, had easy access to the CFO, and was able to name whatever resources I needed. I also had my pick of assignments. Funny how easy it is to succeed when you can choose your assignments and your team and have access to all the people who can help you.

Another time I had been labeled as a star, I had taken over a poor-performing department, created new services, and turned it around. One of our tasks was to communicate our new services, and my team came up with several creative ways to advertise all our changes, including putting "commercials" on the corporate television channel. At the time, I was also known to coach people outside my direct responsibility. People would come to me for advice or ideas, and sometimes it was apparent that another person's work had my fingerprints on it. I was labeled as creative and supportive, a good label to have, except that whenever someone came up with an innovative idea, I got credit for it. People started attributing all sorts of accomplishments to my coaching or advice, even when I wasn't remotely involved. I also noticed that my colleagues were very forgiving of my mistakes. Forgetting to bring my report to a meeting was just a by-product of my creativity, while for the "dogs," that was just further proof of their incompetence.

The labeling effect is another cognitive bias that is widely documented by psychologists and other neuroscientists. Rüdiger Pohl, in the book *Cognitive Illusions*, defines the labeling effect as occurring when "a specific label is affixed to a stimulus and exerts its distorting influence in subsequent judgment or recall." In other aspects of life, we are very careful not to stereotype or label others. This is especially true in our schools. Two of the most famous experiments on labeling and its consequences were done with schoolchildren. One famous experiment was made into a popular documentary called *A Class Divided*. In this experiment, a teacher divided her class by eye color. One day, the blue-eyed children were told that they were superior to brown-eyed children, and as a result, they behaved that way, even performing better on tests. Then the teacher reversed the situation, putting brown-eyed children on top, resulting in the brown-eyed children performing better than the blue-eyed ones.

Another experiment with schoolchildren involved deceiving their teachers into thinking a certain number of kids were early academic bloomers, having scored high on an exam to determine academic readiness. In reality, the subset was randomly chosen. However, at the end of the school year, the children in this randomly chosen subset outperformed their peers. Both of these experiments show that labels result in different treatment, even when there is no discerning basis for the labels. Because of these types of experiments, children are no longer segregated by apparent ability in the elementary classroom. Other studies have shown that once something is labeled a certain way, we perceive it to be that way, even when the original label is proven to be false. We filter our perception based on labels. The impact of labeling is a self-fulfilling prophecy.

While our educators have been fully versed in the adverse effects of identifying and segregating high performers, this practice is touted by many talent management consultants to be critical to an organization's success. You have to identify and reward your stars because they are the future of your company! This means that businesses have processes and policies in place to specifically label and stereotype employees, not according to race or religion, but according to a number that is often biased by race, religion, gender, and other factors. A practice eschewed everywhere else in life is a talent management best practice! Besides being subject to the biases of the manager, the problem with the rating system is that employees must be labeled and sorted at a particular moment in time. Although a manager may be privy to the entire work history of an employee, that manager is compelled to give her own honest and often biased assessment of the employee. That's the role of a manager. The manager is supposed to evaluate, aka judge, the employee. Therefore, whatever moment in time in which you are asked to do the assessment has the potential of providing a label that can stick for a lengthy duration, especially if the employee doesn't change jobs or managers.

▷ Sometimes the A players are alienated by this system, too

The purpose of the sorting is to find the employees with leadership potential so they can be groomed for the next management levels. The logic is that because this step is so important, it is worth the risk of alienating everyone else to lavish attention and resources on the A players to help them excel and keep them with the company. Theoretically, in the talent war, losing A players has a huge cost to the company. My experience at two different "best-company-to-work-for" Fortune 100 corporations has been that these policies can alienate the high performers as well. The worst example occurred when I was part of a women's leadership program. My business unit had particularly poor representation of women and minorities in leadership positions, and it had instituted some initiatives to address the problem. At one point, I was given the name of a senior-ranking woman who could potentially act as my mentor. We arranged a time to meet so she could share some career advice with me. Imagine my surprise when she spent the meeting complaining about the current leadership and told me to look for a job elsewhere if I wanted to advance my career!

The career path to the leadership ranks in our business unit was through Marketing, and this woman had moved up through Marketing into a country management position. Recognized as a potential leader, she was chosen for a development opportunity and asked to lead a global diversity project. This project lasted about eighteen months. By coincidence, while she was working on this initiative to improve the diversity of the leadership team, her male colleagues were slowly moving into positions of more responsibility and gaining more general management experience. In a stroke of bad luck the president had resigned, opening up slots at the top and offering the rare chance for senior-level promotions. When she returned to her normal job eighteen months later, all her peers had been promoted into superior positions, while she basically had nowhere to go. She couldn't move ahead until she gained more general management experience. Her career had been derailed by her leadership development opportunity. When we spoke, she was coleading another global initiative, not a position in line for advancement. She was also actively job hunting outside the company. While her situation was incredibly unlucky, similar situations occurred with other people participating in A-player development opportunities. Another woman from Marketing found that her whole management team had moved into positions with other business units while she was on a development opportunity, and she had a difficult time returning at all. She had to go back to the same position she left a full two and a half years earlier. Her colleagues who weren't being developed had all been promoted beyond her. Another A player found herself without a job after her department was restructured. When a group of us formed a women's leadership network, the first piece of advice imparted was "Don't accept a development opportunity."

My own experience with development opportunities at a different company wasn't much better. My development opportunity was to lead a Windows/Office/Explorer upgrade. Not only did I have no experience with this type of project, I had no interest in it nor was I suited to it. I honestly don't understand the thinking behind the decision. The work required an inventory of everything on everyone's PC and then rigorous testing of how these programs interacted with the upgraded software. The success of this type of project depends on paying attention to all the details, testing everything thoroughly, and documenting it all. Although I wouldn't be doing the testing and documenting myself, it would be my responsibility to ensure it was all done properly. I've already told you about some of my weaknesses, one of which is details. I also have a pretty good memory, which means I'm not in the habit of writing things down. What I'm bad at: details, checklists, following checklists, documenting details, and organizing details, all the skills needed on this assignment. Why on earth would I be asked to lead a project so completely ill suited to my strengths? I suspect someone thought I needed to develop "detail-orientation" skills, one of the leadership competencies. This ended up being my last straw, and I left the company after it had invested in sending me to a leadership training program.

I realize that these are just anecdotes from my career and not a statistically sound study of high-potential programs, but these involved two world-class companies that alienated some of their A players through the use of special development programs. I'm sure this practice is useful in some situations, but there is no guarantee that this is the best way to treat your A players. However, this is currently considered to be a leadership development best practice, to be imitated by all companies wanting to groom future leaders. The precept is that finding and developing your A players is worth the risk of alienating everyone else, but A players can be alienated by this practice, too.

▷ The Peter Principle is not a joke

The other purpose of the labeling system is to determine who is worthy of promotion. In most companies, you have to demonstrate superior performance at your job to get promoted into another one. The underlying assumption is that people who perform well at one job are likely to perform well at another. If you don't demonstrate mastery of your position, you are either stuck there or you have to update your résumé. If you look at this practice holistically, an organization keeps its poor and medium performers in the same jobs while promoting high performers until they no longer perform well. This is the Peter Principle. We all joke about the Peter Principle, but it does exist, and it ensures that you have the *least* effective workforce possible. For those of you unfamiliar with the Peter Principle, it was first written about in 1969 in a book by Dr. Lawrence Peter and Raymond Hull. The principle states, *In a hierarchy every employee tends to rise to his level of incompetence.* Basically, if you are competent in your job, you eventually get promoted to a new one and so on until you become incompetent and are no longer eligible for promotion.

This principle results in an organization where most people are incompetent at their jobs. In fact, three students from Universita di Catania built an agent-based computer model to simulate this principle to see whether it was true. Using 160 positions in a pyramidal hierarchy, they assigned ages and levels of competence to their agents and created open positions by firing incompetent agents and retiring old agents. Then they tested three different rules to move agents to the next level: the most competent, the least competent, or a random choice. They also simulated two different ways of determining the new competency after a move: randomly assigning a new one or using the old one with a random fudge factor. Promoting the most competent worked well only when the agents retained a high competency after a move. An organization has to be sure that its best performers will be the best performers in all jobs for this practice to be effective. When competence changed after a move, promoting the best had the effect of spreading incompetence through the organization. The least risky strategy under both competence change scenarios was to alternate promoting your worst and best employees! Just promoting people at random also worked well in both scenarios. These latter two methods allowed people to move out of jobs when they couldn't perform, which is the only way to make sure the Peter Principle doesn't apply. (Some companies require frequent job moves to prevent the Peter Principle from occurring, but I'm not sure that works. That policy randomly opens up new jobs for a random selection, so the probability of getting a job you are good at is low.)

▷ We are pushing people toward mediocrity

The best way to deal with "incompetence" is to move that person out of that job. Yet this conflicts with the recommended treatment for C players; they need to be coached to improve and then demonstrate improvement or else be let go. (I guess being let go is one way to move someone out of a job.) Some companies have formal performance plans with action items and probationary periods that must be completed before the C players can be treated like regular employees again. In companies that don't have these formal punitive policies, the informal word of mouth about internal job candidates can have the same effect. The harshest treatment of C players is the aforementioned rank and yank or automatic firing of the bottom tier.

Professional services firms have a similar policy called "up or out": if you don't get promoted within a certain time frame, you have to leave. Fortunately, this policy seems to have waned in popularity in recent years. At one consulting firm where I worked, the HR department instituted an "up or out" policy that we nicknamed the "up and out" policy. Basically, every year the bottom 10 percent were culled, including those who did not meet the promotion timeline. Senior consultants promoted to manager positions were required to sell client work in addition to managing project teams. Typically, new managers already had the project management experience needed, but the selling aspect was a new job responsibility. In this new role, some of the best consultants floundered initially, as it takes some time to learn how to sell work and to develop the relationships. However, with this cull-the-bottom-10-percent policy, they got fired before they could learn the new job. We were systematically culling our best talent upon promotion! This policy was abandoned after a couple of years but not without a loss of high performers. In addition to those who were fired, consultants on the cusp of promotion left in droves because they didn't want it to happen to them. Funny how people rarely submit passively to punitive HR policies!

So treating the A players like superstars or pushing them into development programs has its risks. Culling the C players also has its risks. What about the B players, the bulk of the organization? The recommended treatment is to give A and C players most of your attention and just affirm to B players that they are valued and offer them development as needed. In other words, those stuck in the middle are, well, stuck in the middle. Isn't the real impact of the differing ABC treatment to push everyone toward the middle? Cs get let go or coached to B. As are developed and promoted until they reach B, where they receive little attention. Only a few will continue to be A players all the way to the top. The Bs are left alone unless they move to A or C. The ultimate result of all these talent management policies is to push everyone to the middle of the curve where they get no attention, thus ensuring a mediocre organization!

This whole ABC player philosophy confounds me. To be honest, much of the talent management philosophy confounds me. Talent or potential is a constant. You either have talent or you don't. Talent is not the same as performance; only a subset of high performers have talent. However, high performance is a hallmark of having talent. High performers should have a solid track record of performance, except when they take risks and fail. So their performance should be variable and include failures. A history of failure is the hallmark of a poor performer. Poor performers can be coached to improve and even become high performers. Performance can be developed. Potential or talent can also be developed—except that talent is a constant that you either have or you don't. Managers should be rated on how well they develop their employees, but managers should not get penalized for poor-performing employees because it is the responsibility of the employees to meet their objectives. Am I the only person who is utterly confused by this conflicting logic?

This is what I do know about performance in the workplace:

1. Performance is conditional. Although a great variety exists in the abilities and achievements of people, most people can achieve high performance under the right conditions, and most people will perform poorly given adverse conditions. Hence, assuming that high performers will always be high performers in any job and any circumstance is just not true—ditto for the poor performers.

2. Poor performance is usually not due to incompetence. Although I've met my share of incompetent people, most

performance issues are due to poor job fit, poor relationship fit with peers or manager, or poor culture fit with the company. Only a small percentage is due to the general incompetence of the employee.

3. Labels are a self-fulfilling prophecy. High performers are typically given more attention, more resources, and better opportunities, thereby enhancing their chances for success. Poor performers are usually put on a tight leash and given limited resources and opportunities, thereby limiting their chances for success. Average performers are only expected to be average and given very little attention. Given that most performance management systems with ratings demand that the bulk of employees perform at the average level, most of the employees will perform at the average level. In fact, this is what many HR departments demand.

4. The Peter Principle really exists. People will be promoted out of jobs they excel in until they land a job they don't excel in. People in ill-suited jobs typically are left to their own devices to find their way out of that position.

5. People like to control their own destiny, especially high-performing individuals. Plunking people in projects or jobs not of their own choosing is a punishment, not a reward. Encouraging someone to leave his comfort zone is very different from demanding that he do so.

▷ Fit the jobs to the people, not the people to the boxes

With all the focus on putting employees in A, B, or C boxes, companies miss the conversation that has the most impact on the most people—job fit. While we spend hours rating people on a curve, arguing who gets $10 more in an annual pay increase, and nitpicking over the skills needed for development, we rarely ever talk with employees about their fit with their current positions. In my thirty-year career, I have never gone to a meeting where managers or anyone else got together to determine how the company could get more employees to be high performing. I've never been in a meeting where we discussed development opportunities for average-performing employees. I have never been in a meeting where the agenda was employee job fit. Sometimes this discussion is held for the A players or for senior levels of leadership, though often without their attendance. Most companies leave this conversation for the development part of the performance appraisal meeting between manager and employee. Yet managers on their own are powerless to move people into new positions and even less likely to recognize when they are part of the performance problem.

If you think about it, in management, this is the most important conversation there is. How do I get the most out of my organization? How do I get more people to be high performing? The answer is to help more people find their sweet spot—that confluence of the right work, the right people, and the right skills. It may not exist for everyone, but if you don't try to find it, you never will. Yet I have never had this conversation at work.

Instead, we spend our time arguing over the performance rating, begging managers to follow the curve, dreaming up development opportunities for others without their participation, documenting succession plans—even developing a human resource contingency plan if half the leadership team dies in a fiery plane crash—but nowhere near enough time on trying to bring out the best in most of our employees. Here's what we need to do to start: Abandon the labels. Eliminate the bell curves. Stop performing talent management on people. Allow anyone who wants to change positions to easily change positions. And above all, start having conversations with employees and their managers about how to find the best job fit.

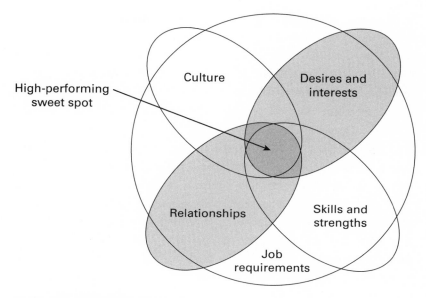

Figure 4 **Job fit sweet spot**

I use the sweet spot diagram in figure 4 to explain how I understand the basic components of a good job fit. Keep in mind that this is my made-up model. (Hey, I'm a consultant. What did you expect?) The first two are environmental—fit with the company culture and relationship fit with the manager and peers. The second two are internal to the employee, which is why the employee has to be part of the conversation. The job should be a fit with the person's skills and interests. This effort won't result in a sweet spot for everyone, but imagine what a difference it would make if you found it for just half the organization. Instead of all the time spent trying to fit people into boxes, it is spent actually doing something of value—using your employees' talents.

Having the job fit conversation solves many of the problems of talent management. It assumes everyone has some level of talent that can be developed. Talent and performance can be the same thing. Because no one is graded, the meetings and outcomes don't have to be secret. Employees can succeed or fail without being labeled. Failures can be addressed quickly with a move and without shame. More importantly, rather than everyone else being responsible for a person's career development, the employees can take ownership of their own careers. They can request a move. They can come to the meetings prepared to discuss their abilities and interests and participate in finding their best fit. Managers don't have to be saddled with the responsibility of employees' career development, which is typically beyond their span of control. Instead, they can concentrate on improving their employees' performance, which is within their span of control. Another advantage of changing the conversation from performance or talent to fit is that if a proper fit for a person cannot be found, it is less personal, less degrading, and less contentious to be let go because of poor fit than poor performance.

Another box that needs to be thrown away for this to work is the job description. Sometimes there are very good reasons to write a job description. I have done them myself. However, the practice of writing up the job and all its requirements and then looking for a person who fits the box is much less productive than matching the work to the people. And here is where Einstein makes another great example. In Einstein's day, if you were to apply for the job of physicist, it usually meant an experimental physicist. The norm was for scientists to work in labs and conduct experiments. Einstein conducted what he called "thought experiments," not physical ones. Although Einstein was not the first theoretical physicist, after his fame it became the norm to choose work in theoretical physics or experimental physics. He created a new job description!

7

Great Leaders Don't Fit the Models

Steve Jobs Failed My Leadership Competencies

▷ **The ongoing debate: What traits make a leader?**

Now that we have eliminated the sorting, ranking, and labeling, we have a very big problem. We have no way to identify the future leaders of the company. Without a leadership pipeline in place, a company will find itself without competent leaders and will crash and burn in a fiery blaze of mediocre management only to become the next Harvard Business School case study on what not to do. Continuing the legacy of the talent war, talent management consultants will often cite this potential leadership crisis as the reason for all those HR systems. Without them, how do you identify those A players who will become the future leadership of your company? Let me put on my own consulting hat for a moment. That person whom nobody knows, does her job well but sticks to her own responsibilities—probably not a potential leader. That other person, the one everyone knows, who volunteers for everything, and who loves leading teams and projects—yep, that's the one with the potential. There you go. I have assessed leadership potential. That will be $2,500, please.

I apologize for being flippant. I realize that this is an important business concern. It's just that so many leadership consultants and coaches and gurus, leadership assessments, and leadership development programs are urging you to develop specific leadership competencies, it's hard to separate the hype and hypotheses from sound practices. I know in a previous chapter I said I wasn't going to make the distinction between management and leadership, but in this chapter I want to talk about what is currently billed as "leadership development." In many companies, leadership development applies to everyone, meaning that everyone is expected to learn a certain level of leadership skills, making the distinction between manager and leader even harder to make. The premise behind leadership development programs is that good leadership consists of a specific set of capabilities that can be learned. I use the word "capabilities" because some of these are personal attributes, like self-awareness, rather than a typical skill, like "communicates clearly." A lot is going on in this premise. First, it is assumed that leadership ability can be broken down into its component parts. In reverse, this assumption means that all good leaders possess the same set of skills and attributes. The second part of this premise is that these skills and attributes are not necessarily innate but can be acquired with effort.

So what are the attributes of a good leader?

Winston Churchill, Mahatma Gandhi, Martin Luther King Jr., Abraham Lincoln, Ulysses Grant, Theodore Roosevelt, Douglas MacArthur, Dwight Eisenhower, and Thomas Jefferson are all considered great leaders. What do these people have in common? Charisma or charm? Neither Grant nor Jefferson was considered to be charismatic. In fact, Jefferson hated public speaking, wasn't particularly adept at it, and sent his State of the Union messages to Congress to be read even though his two predecessors had addressed Congress in person. Gandhi, MLK, and Lincoln were respected for their sense of humility, but there was nothing humble about Churchill, Roosevelt, or MacArthur. MacArthur had a reputation for being dramatic, while Eisenhower and Grant were laid back personalities. Both Churchill and Grant battled with alcohol abuse, while Jefferson had different vices, dying woefully in debt and unable to free his slaves. Lincoln and Gandhi, in contrast, had upstanding moral characters. What about their upbringing? Some were rich; some were poor. What about vision? MLK certainly had one, as did Jefferson. Were Eisenhower and Grant visionaries? Not really. It's not obvious to me what traits these leaders have in common.

Fortunately, even more so than management, leadership is a topic that has been studied for centuries. Starting with Machiavelli, people throughout history have been obsessed with what makes a great leader. It's a hot topic in the business world as well. Leadership gurus, books, and models abound, so let's look at what the experts say about leadership attributes. I'm going to look at more recent experts than Machiavelli because I think our ideas have changed considerably since the Renaissance. Once again, I pulled my dusty books from the shelves and discovered that I have even more leadership books than management books. Fortunately, none of them is 609 pages long.

My first leadership book was a gift of a signed copy of Warren Bennis's *On Becoming a Leader*, first published in 1989. Bennis was one of the first people I remember being considered a leadership guru. His ingredients for leadership are a guiding vision, passion, integrity, trustworthiness, curiosity, and daring. Bennis emphasizes the ability of a great leader to shape himself in the way he wants to be and, as a result, shape his environment. In the book's introduction, Bennis sums up his research on leadership: "No leader sets out to be a leader per se, but rather to express himself freely and fully. That is, leaders have no interest in proving themselves, but an abiding interest in expressing themselves. The difference is crucial, for it's the difference between being driven,

as too many people are today, and leading, as too few people do."
That's a very humble view of leadership. Most people I know in
leadership positions are there because they strove to be.

My second leadership book from around the same time is
John W. Gardner's *On Leadership*. At the time, Gardner was
famous as a leadership guru, but I rarely hear his name bandied
about today, probably because he died in 2002 and so many others are vying for attention. John Gardner was the secretary of
Health, Education, and Welfare under Lyndon Johnson and
became noteworthy for several landmark federal programs,
including Medicare; the Elementary and Secondary Education
Act of 1965, which redefined the federal role in education; and
the Corporation for Public Broadcasting. Gardner described six
things that leaders did differently from managers. Leaders

1. Think longer term
2. See the bigger picture
3. Are able to influence others outside their immediate sphere
   of control
4. Value the nonrational, unconscious, and intangible aspects
   of behavior
5. Exhibit political skills to deal with multiple constituencies
6. Question the status quo

This is a different take from Bennis's research. Bennis focuses
on internal qualities that describe self-actualization, while many
of Gardner's elements have to do with how a person relates to the
external world—strategic thinking, political savvy, influence.

Jim Collins is a more recent and world-renowned business
management guru who has written several business best sell-
ers. In his book *Good to Great*, Collins describes a number of
characteristics that set great companies apart and enable them

to achieve lasting greatness. One of these characteristics is that they are headed by a Level 5 leader. A Level 5 leader possesses a unique combination of personal humility and professional will. This means that they credit successes to others and to external factors, while taking the blame for failures themselves. They are realistic about the challenges facing their companies but are committed to overcoming them. They are able to subjugate their egos to a higher purpose, having achieved this ability either through intense self-reflection or a traumatic life event. Collins makes the distinction between Level 5 leaders and Level 4 leaders, who tend to be egotistical and sometimes charismatic people capable of motivating people toward a vision. Level 4 leaders can achieve remarkable change, but Level 5 leaders build great organizations that outlast their leadership.

In addition to his leadership styles model, Daniel Goleman has created a list of traits of successful leaders that aligns with his emotional intelligence theory. His must-have leadership traits are self-awareness, self-regulation, motivation, empathy, and social skills. While his traits are different from Warren Bennis's, they both describe leadership in terms of internal capabilities, as does Jim Collins. I call this focus on internal traits "the self-actualized leader model." Another famous management guru and also a professor at the Harvard Business School, John Kotter, assigns the role of change agent to a successful leader. He describes leadership as setting direction, aligning people, and providing motivation. Like John Gardner's model, this is more of an action model or what you have to do or be able to do as a leader. Okay, my head is starting to hurt. I still have a bunch more material—Peter Drucker, Stephen Covey, Peter Senge. As a writer, I have a general rule: if it is boring to write, then it will be even more boring to read. So I am stopping.

My point is that numerous leadership gurus have conducted copious research, and all have their models of what traits or actions are required to be a leader. Although some of these traits are similar, there really is no consensus on exactly what those traits are. However, all the leadership gurus agree that leaders can be made. Therefore, leadership development is a plausible concept. Keep in mind, though, that most of these people make a living at leadership development, so there is just a small conflict of interest. One other thing I've gleaned from the research is that none of these gurus mention more than a handful of traits. So far, Bennis's list is longest with six traits.

▷ If traits don't make a leader, what are leadership assessments assessing?

Now I want to compare my synopsis of leadership theory to what is being practiced in industry. Leadership assessments are a booming business. In fact, when I searched through my desk to find the assessment done on me, I was shocked to discover that I had been assessed not once but three times with three different tools. I remembered only one particular assessment, not because of the insights I got from it, but because of its length. I was assessed in twenty-four competency areas. This thing is pages and pages long. I wouldn't have minded so much if I had been the only one filling it out, but my manager, my direct reports, and a group of my peers had to do this for me—and not once but three times (although the two other tools were shorter). A couple of years later, I was asked by two separate people to do the same lengthy assessment of them. I remember I thought it would never end. Although I really wanted to do my best and give them helpful information, I had no meaningful answer for many of the questions and ended up just giving them "average," especially in the latter part of the assessment when I became tired. That gave me tremendous insight into my own assessment as I tended to rate average in the latter part of my questionnaire.

The result of the assessment was an identification of my strengths and my weaknesses. With those isolated, I developed an action plan that would leverage my strengths and develop my weak areas. Reviewing this a decade later, I laughed at my action plan for my weaknesses. My top "leadership derailer" was my lack of organization. Listed underneath, I have steps for getting more organized. I laughed because this report is sitting atop one of several piles of paper that have spilled onto the floor from the top of my desk, which is completely covered with files and books and other piles. Oops. Guess I didn't achieve that one. Now I can never become a great leader.

These leadership competencies aren't just part of assessments that employees take for training or advancement. They are now written into many performance reviews. In addition to being rated on goal achievement, employees are rated on a list of attributes. If you lack some of these skill areas, you get a black mark on your review, so people try to make sure that they have attained a certain level of competence in all of them. In fact, many companies have training programs in place to ensure a certain level of competency in all these attributes, hence, the mastery of twenty-odd competencies to be a successful leader. You may think that this lengthy list of traits is an exception. Along with my old leadership assessments, I also dusted off an old performance review. (You may be gaining insight into the origins of my piles of papers.) It includes several pages where one is rated on one's leader behaviors. It has thirty-four behaviors divided into eight overarching categories, for example:

- Sustain focus on performance
    Seizes opportunities to improve the business
    Is guided by high standards
    Sets the right priorities
    Is oriented to our customers

- Create an inclusive environment
    Is open to new ideas
    Includes colleagues
    Ensures managers do the same

- Encourage open discussion/debate
    Listens actively
    Encourages contribution
    Accepts criticism
    Skillfully manages meetings and discussions
    Communicates effectively

- Manage change
    Anticipates strategically
    Takes initiative
    Plans for better ways to operate
    Empowers people to act
    Trains change agents
    Seeks better practices

- Develop people
    Yada, yada, yada

- Align across the company
    Yada, yada, yada

- Foster innovation and creativity
    Etc., etc.,

- Demonstrate strategic agility
    More of the same

A friend shared the leadership competency model she helped develop for a very large organization. It is in the shape of a circle and it has four major components—thoughts, results, personal, and people—similar to the breakdown of competencies in the

Successful Manager's Handbook. It has twenty subsets of skills, which are then broken out into another layer of skills, too numerous for me to readily count. This type of model has worked its way into conventional management practices. It is now assumed that to be a good leader, you need to "demonstrate mastery" of anywhere between twenty and forty skills going by the name of "leadership competencies."

But what about Steve Jobs?

Seriously, Steve Jobs would have failed all my leadership competency assessments. Everything I have read about Steve Jobs—how he treated employees, friends, and even his caregivers—makes him seem like a real jerk. Yet no matter how much his mean behavior violates our image of a good leader, he was undeniably a great leader. He built three companies in total, two of which are amazing companies with unsurpassed records of success—Apple and Pixar—and created whole new business models and industries, such as iTunes and the iPod, iPad, and iPhone. He radically changed the way people communicate, surf the web, and listen to music. According to Jim Collins, a Level 5 leader is one who can create a sustainable company. Steve Jobs surpassed that criterion by creating whole new industries. When he died, he received an outpouring of grief that is usually reserved for entertainers and politicians. He had followers all across the globe. But he certainly wasn't humble. His people skills were sorely lacking, too, especially on the empathy side. Maybe Steve Jobs was a unique exception, but what about

- Larry Ellison of Oracle?
- Carly Fiorina of HP?
- Meg Whitman of eBay and HP?
- Neutron Jack Welch of GE?
- Michael Eisner of Disney?

All these CEOs have been described as either heartless, aggressive, brusque, micromanaging, or tyrannical. The eminence of Steve Jobs as the ideal CEO has set off a debate in the business press about whether good leaders really need to have people skills or empathy. Recently, an article in *Forbes* called "Why (Some) Psychopaths Make Great CEOs," stated that about 4 percent of CEOs are psychopaths as compared to 1 percent of the general population, and those aggressive and unsympathetic qualities are what makes them successful. The *New York Times* published an article called "Addictive Personality? You Might Be a Leader" in a similar vein about a large proportion of CEOs having addictive personalities, which makes them more obsessive and risk taking than the rest of us. Needing the constant adrenaline rush, they are not satisfied with mundane achievements.

Manfred F. R. Kets de Vries, another leadership guru, has identified narcissism as a common trait among CEOs and other successful leaders. The clinical profile of a narcissist is a male whose childhood was dominated by a devoted mother while his father was either absent or distant. According to the Mayo Clinic website, "Narcissistic personality disorder is a mental disorder in which people have an inflated sense of their own importance and a deep need for admiration. Those with narcissistic personality disorder believe that they're superior to others and have little regard for other people's feelings." Michael Maccoby also writes extensively about narcissistic leaders, especially their strengths and weaknesses. Of all the personality types, narcissists seem to be the most able to exhibit the daring and confidence needed to take the big risks of anticipating new industries and creating breakthrough products. Of all the "traits" that make a good leader, the one that seems most highly correlated with leadership success is narcissism. Therefore, instead of being rated on various social abilities, leadership assessments should really be asking about the relationship you had with your mother and your father.

But what about

- Sam Walton of Walmart?
- Lou Gerstner of IBM?
- Warren Buffett of Berkshire Hathaway?
- Herb Kelleher of Southwest Airlines?
- Walt Disney?

None of these famous and successful leaders are known to be egomaniacal, people-using narcissists. So which is it? Are good leaders narcissists or self-actualized achievers or visionary doers? The experts don't seem to have reached any consensus, so let's ask one of our leaders, the one who started this whole debate. In a 2003 interview for *60 Minutes*, Steve Jobs said, "My model for business is The Beatles. They were four guys who kept each other's kind of negative tendencies in check. They balanced each other, and the total was greater than the sum of the parts. That's how I see business: great things in business are never done by one person; they're done by a team of people."

▷We use teams because one person can't be good at everything

All these leadership competencies are nice to talk about, but in reality they don't make a good or successful leader. In reality, people adapt to strengths and weaknesses, their own and those of others. To compensate for their own weaknesses, leaders surround themselves with others who possess the skills they lack. This allows the whole team to emphasize their strengths. The other interesting point is that followers adapt to the weaknesses of their leaders, if given enough reason to.

Steve Wozniak built the first Apple computers. It wasn't the two Steves working in a garage building a PC. Woz did the technical work, and Jobs did all the marketing and sales. Jobs's biggest contribution was that he recognized the market opportunity for the personal computer and persuaded Woz to start a company with him. Jobs didn't create the graphical user interface that set Apple apart. He saw it at Xerox Parc and recognized its potential. The same with Pixar. He didn't create Pixar. He bought it from Lucasfilm because he saw its potential. Jobs, celebrated for the design of his products, also wasn't a designer. He appreciated good design, so he hired good designers. His team tolerated his obnoxious behavior because he brought an extraordinary talent to the table—his ability to recognize and exploit potential, both that of good ideas and that of good people. If Steve Jobs did not have this talent, no one would have tolerated his egotism and perfectionism.

When you read stories about great companies and great leaders, the common thread is that the leaders didn't do it by themselves. All these CEOs have had a team of people with diverse skills working for them. The reality of the situation is that no leadership formula or model works for everyone. Each person has unique skills and qualities, and the point is to maximize those while mitigating the weaknesses, either through training, compensating, or building a team. When I look back at my disorganization as my "derailer" behavior, I find it completely irrelevant. I have no interest in filing papers or keeping my desk neat. What a waste of time. I am fortunate that I have always had someone working for me that was good at filing or just took on the task of keeping me organized. Although my lack of organization has been a topic of jokes and playful derision, no one has ever seriously complained to me about it. I received a low score on a sheet of paper that somehow was supposed to dictate how I could improve as a person. A piece of paper can't know who I am. Because I have lots of other talents to offer—like being able to bring out the best in people, solve problems, and manage workloads—that are so much more important, my subordinates, peers, and managers are happy to deal with my messy desk.

People adapt. That is the one thing humans excel at doing. We adapt to our surroundings, and we adapt to other people. We can forgive deficiencies in someone's personality if that person brings something else to the table. That's key. You need to have some kind of talent. However, lots of talented people are not leaders. What makes a leader rise to the top is some kind of drive or will to succeed. Narcissists are driven by the need for acclaim. Self-actualized leaders are driven by their passion or desire to make the world a better place. Visionaries are driven by the need to realize their vision. Something makes them work hard, persevere in their goals, and inspire others to follow them. Whether that drive is internal or external, altruistic or egotistic, is irrelevant. Drive without any requisite talent probably doesn't result in much. But that talent could be almost anything when you build a team of talented people. So why on earth are we demanding that our employees develop competence in a laundry list of skills that have no real relevance to leadership ability? Even more ironic, it is really easy to assess "drive" to choose employees for leadership programs. Let them apply to join, but make the application process very rigorous. Only those with drive will fulfill the application requirements.

▷ Trying to be good at everything is the way to achieve mediocrity

When I discuss, well, rant, about leader competencies to my friends who are human resources consultants, they often try to convince me that these competence models provide a lot of good for employees. They are usually the basis for employee training programs. I agree that employee development and training are worthwhile. In fact, a great deal of empirical evidence shows that companies that invest in their employees, especially in training and development, outperform those that don't. However, I've come to believe that requiring all employees to develop a certain level of competence in thirty skill areas and attend corporate-sponsored training classes to do so is actually inhibiting real leadership development. And here is where I need to apologize. Back in the early '90s, I was on the forefront of this whole competency effort, and I actually helped create one of these in-depth competence models. I'm sorry.

In 1994, I took a position in my consulting company's internal training department. At the time, the only program we had was a two-week new-hire orientation boot camp called "Gemini Skills Workshop" or GSW. This program was generally recognized as a best practice within the company for a number of reasons. It was built around a real client case study; it focused on a few skills, which were practiced ad nauseam; and throughout the two weeks, participants received extensive coaching from the facilitators and feedback from the other participants. Overall, GSW was an intense bonding experience where the company culture, jargon, and values were inculcated. One of the strengths of this program was that it concentrated on a few vital consulting skills, like meeting facilitation, brainstorming techniques, and client interviewing. GSW's purpose was for every consultant to be useful on the first day of a project. We created a road map of consulting skills and documented the expected level of competence upon completion of the GSW. This way, project managers knew exactly what skills they could count on new hires having and assign them accordingly. To keep the program up to date, the training function would periodically survey the company leaders to determine what skills should be emphasized. Although we occasionally introduced new material depending on needs, the basic skills rarely changed.

As the company grew and we embarked on the business transformation strategy, our leadership realized that we would need to provide more training to our consultants. This was especially important because to fill our pipeline, we were hiring more candidates out of school and fewer experienced hires. Because GSW worked so well, the leaders wanted a continuation of that type of training. The idea of Gemini University (GU, for short) was born. Now we needed to know what to teach.

We took the concept of competencies and applied it to the company as a whole. By now, the word "competency" was fully rooted in the business lexicon, and we worked with the various practice areas to develop competencies and training for their consultants. It was a huge undertaking with everyone slotted into a development track based on industry (financial services, manufacturing, etc.), practice (operations, strategy, IT, etc.), or functional expertise (supply chain, sales and marketing, etc.). The end product was a list of required competencies by position and the mandatory training to achieve them. Although the head of operations decided that everyone in the supply chain function should get certified through APICS (American Production and Inventory Control Society), most of the classes were in-house through GU. The first GU was held in New Jersey, and it was deemed a huge success due to the number of attendees. This had to be a good thing, right? People were getting training in skills they needed for the future success of the company.

At first I couldn't put my finger on it, but the atmosphere of the university program was different from that of the orientation boot camp. Of course, it was ten times larger, but the GSW participants seemed happy to be there. I can't say the same for all the GU attendees. We continued to hold the classes, twice a year, alternating between Paris and New Jersey. I began teaching a course, and over the few years that I taught, I noted that most of the people in my class did not want to be there. When I asked a few why they seemed resentful, they explained that this was their valuable training time, and it was being wasted on topics they didn't want to learn. Other consulting companies sent their consultants to conferences or to external courses of their own choosing, but at Gemini, your only real option was internal training classes, and a mandatory training track limited your options even more.

I had worked in supply chain and began to talk with my colleagues about why they were disgruntled over the new competency development track. Many of our outstanding consultants had previously worked in supply chains at major companies. They saw absolutely no need for an APICS certification. How can passing a multiple-choice test be better than ten to fifteen years of real-world experience? They were interested in learning about a new software called "SAP" and another new development called "e-commerce." Gradually, they left for other consulting companies, leaving behind those with little experience who needed the certification and had never heard of SAP or e-commerce. Unfortunately, while we were so busy training our consultants on large-scale business transformation skills, we totally missed that the economy had improved, clients didn't want or need large-scale change, Y2K was a huge area of concern, and this new thing called the "Internet" was taking off.

Although developing competencies seems like a great idea, in execution on a large scale, it is an attempt at standardizing people. Think about this. You analyze the skills or competencies that you think you need. You codify these on a piece of paper or computer system. You develop training around these competencies and send all your people through these classes over the course of several years. First, you are training all your people in exactly the same skills, in exactly the same way with the result being that they all think and act the same. You are systematically embedding mediocrity by requiring an average competence in everything from everyone. Secondly, the scale of the program prohibits one from changing the competencies on a regular basis. So now you are embedding a static skill set. Thirdly, there is no room for innovation, creativity, or originality in this model. Although the original idea behind developing core competencies was to compete for the future, what happens is that you are no longer able to gain insight into the new competencies you may need in the future. If you are not letting people pursue their own interests and learn exotic and crazy new ideas, how will you know that the future requires a whole different set of competencies? Innovation can take place only in an environment that encourages diverse thinking, an influx of new ideas, and pursuit of personal passions. Plus, the assumption upon which this whole system is built is faulty. Many of these models describe leadership competencies, the skills required to become a good leader in your chosen field. Yet no one actually knows what competencies make a good leader.

▷ There is no recipe or checklist for self-actualization

Let's get back to the self-actualization school of leadership. How does anyone achieve self-actualization without pursuing her own interests? Look at what shaped Steve Jobs. He had an interest in computers that he pursued on his own. After dropping out of Reed College, he audited a calligraphy class because he thought it was interesting. This sparked his whole obsession with good design. He sought self-enlightenment in India, only to realize that Thomas Edison had a greater impact on the world than any swami. None of the events that shaped Steve Jobs were company or school sanctioned.

When I look at my own career and consider what helped me become a better person and also a better leader, most of those weren't company sanctioned, either. The top item is parenthood. I became a much better manager after having children because I learned how to deal with other people on their terms and not always my own. You can't tell a two-year-old that you're the boss, and he needs to do what you say. I mean, you can, but it won't get you anywhere. Regarding training, the classes that helped me most were on systems dynamics, neurolinguistic programming, and a women's leadership program that stressed the importance of relationships. Only the last one was part of corporate training, and it was a recommended external program, not a mandated one. There is such a big difference between choosing to be there and having to be there.

The last big problem with this attempt at standardizing the workforce is that it inhibits the chance of self-actualization at work. If all your development is through mandatory programs and you get stuck in a job for which you are ill suited, your chances of finding a personal passion at work are slim to none. If you haven't found a personal passion, how can you create a compelling vision for the future that inspires others? Remember our schools of thought on great leaders—self-actualized achievers, visionary doers, or narcissists? If self-actualization and finding your passion have become harder due to rigid competency requirements, who is left? It's scary to think that through the widespread use of talent management systems, companies may now be ensuring that the only people who can rise to the top are the narcissists.

We need to get rid of the laundry list of leadership attributes that employees are required to master. No one really knows what traits make a good leader. Get rid of the copious mandatory training and e-learning classes. Do offer training to your employees, but make it a menu of in-house, external, and "you get to choose" classes. For internal programs, determine a small set of skills, perhaps five, that you would like all your employees to master. You can't ever go wrong with communications skills like coaching, feedback, and conflict resolution. You may consider a brainstorming, problem-solving, or creativity tool. Offer onboarding and new manager training. But encourage employees to seek training and conferences of their own choosing and to learn things no one has ever heard of yet. Encourage everyone to share the new and crazy things they've learned with others. Remember that the reason we work in groups is so that we can benefit from the strengths of others and offset their weaknesses. Not everyone needs to be competent at everything. This is why we work in organizations.

But what about identifying the future leaders of a company and developing that talent? This is still a vital function a company needs to survive. Whether it is called "drive," "passion," "singular pursuit," "ambition," or "a call to a higher purpose," all leaders have a will to succeed. It may be driven by an altruistic goal or by inner narcissism, but leaders all persist in achieving their goals. They are very easy to identify in the workplace. You know—that person who gets things done and volunteers to lead teams, the one whom everyone knows, the go-to person? Yeah, that's the one. And if you can't find enough of those, let your employees apply to leadership programs with the understanding that the application process will be a lot of work. Only the ones with ambition will apply.

That will be $2,500 please. You're welcome.

8

Out of the Boxes, Charts, and Spreadsheets

How to Think Without Consultants

▷ **Management is not a science**

Frederick Taylor, the father of scientific management, was among the very first management consultants and perhaps the first true management guru. His 1911 book, *The Principles of Scientific Management*, was a best seller for several decades, and his ideas influenced the management of many big American corporations. He was famous in his day, giving many lectures, consulting to well-known companies, and providing advice to the government. Perhaps his greatest legacy is that he helped develop the curriculum at the Harvard Business School, where he also lectured. Even today, the ideas of "Taylorism," associated with monitoring and measuring and finding the one optimized way of performing a task, have outlived the man by a century. Matthew Stewart, in his book, *The Management Myth: Why the Experts Keep Getting It Wrong*, said about Taylor, "In place of verifiable data and reproducible methodologies, he provided only anecdotes, embellished with speciously precise numbers and arcane formulas of indeterminate provenance." Apparently, Taylor was full of bull: performing back-of-the-envelope calculations that had no bearing in reality, overestimating benefits, overcharging his clients, and proclaiming the success of his methods by fudging data—providing the blueprint for the modern management consultant.

Taylor is a good example to examine because we have a century of hindsight with which to judge his ideas. While scientific management was all the rage back in the industrial era, the term "Taylorism" today has mostly a pejorative connotation. Like most great thinkers, Taylor had some very useful ideas and some harmful ones. Some of his useful concepts were to

- Analyze work to determine how to do tasks more efficiently
- Train employees rather than leave them to their own devices
- Find tasks that fit employees' capabilities rather than assign jobs willy-nilly
- Give ample rest breaks to prevent both mental and physical fatigue
- Provide incentives to induce workers to produce more

While many of his ideas are still in practice, his name will be forever associated with the rote, obedient, mechanistic approach to work that ruled the assembly lines a century ago. He believed that thinking work should be separated from manual and menial work and that only a few workers were capable of thinking. He thought managers, the thinkers, should design the work and create standards, while the rest of the employees should be subservient to the managers and follow the rigid standards. This methodology had the effect of dehumanizing the workplace and even resulted in a strike at the Watertown Arsenal. He also never factored human variability into his stopwatch experiments. His most famous case involved finding the most efficient way to shovel pig iron. He chose to observe the strongest and biggest operator to determine the most effective methods (and based his benefit calculations on this person's ability) without considering differences in height, strength, or body type. He also asked the laborer to work as fast as he could, a rate that was unsustainable over long durations.

While Taylorism is mostly repudiated today, the idea that businesses can monitor, measure, and optimize their way to success still survives in modern management methods. We still call upon the mantras of the Taylor efficiency movement: "Work smarter, not harder"; "Do more with less." We still believe measurements are the key to management. We still call it "management science." But where Taylor, and many subsequent management consultants, got it wrong is that management is not a science.

The objects of science behave according to the laws of nature because they have no will. Cells divide, planets orbit suns, acids combined with bases explode, and temperature and pressure change the form of elements, all in predictable patterns. None of these objects have a consciousness, an ego, feelings, or a sense of humor. In contrast, the animal kingdom, of which we are part, is constantly surprising us. Who knew that penguins could be homosexual, that bacteria could "speak" complicated languages, or that pigeons could figure out mazes? Yet much of management science assumes that people are rational entities that will behave according to set rules. We know that individual humans do not behave on a purely rational basis, but still we assume that when we put lots of people together, somehow all their irrationalities cancel out each other, and these people behave according to rational formulas. (How many people are required to make the transition from an irrational to a rational body?)

Because management is not actually a science, there are no "answers" and, especially, no business "solutions." Nevertheless, business management theory consists of numerous methodologies and prepackaged solutions that provide step-by-step

instructions on how to be successful. It's ingrained in the thinking of the business world that following a best practice will guarantee success. Very few people even question this assumption.
When data shows that most process reengineering efforts fall
short of their expected benefits, most mergers and acquisitions
fail, and companies with executive incentive compensation plans
tend to underperform those without, instead of questioning the
validity of the theory, executives try to figure out which step they
did wrong so they can try it again. These methods and solutions
are the fad diets and miracle foods of the business world. As long
as business executives keep searching for magical solutions and
guaranteed step-by-step plans, businesses will never develop a
healthy approach to management. Business is not different from
life; it *is* life. What you need to create a healthy business is the
same as what you need to create a healthy life. Fads and step-by-
step methods simply don't work in either case.

A long time ago, I realized that it is much easier to work *with*
human nature than against it. Even more importantly, you are
much more likely to be successful when you work with humans
rather than against them. The underpinning of Taylorism was to
get humans to behave like machines, to act contrary to human
nature. Managers often complain that the reason their initiative
failed was because the employees lacked the discipline to follow
it. Members of a species that created space flight, the Internet,
cartoons, and music videos are not equipped to follow highly
regimented processes or to be purely rational or to sacrifice their
dignity for the sake of corporate policies. Rather than imposing these methods on our workforce in an effort to remove the
human variability, executives need to use these methods as tools
to take advantage of human variability. Instead of trying to take
the humanity out of the workplace, we need to strive to develop
as much humanity as possible. The difference is understanding

that the solutions, methods, and theories are not the truth but someone's perception of how the world works. We can learn from other people's perceptions to broaden our own insight, but we need to recognize there is a good chance that some of their ideas are wrong.

That's the trick, isn't it? How can you discern the good ideas from the bad? It all starts with thinking. Well, it all starts with starting to think. Although I place a lot of the blame for our corporate malaise on consultants, companies are also at fault. Many companies hire consultants to do their thinking for them. Companies will routinely hire consultants to develop their strategies or restructure their companies or determine the feasibility of an acquisition with the result being that people who know nothing about your business are making the most important decisions about your business. One of the biggest flaws of Taylorism was trying to separate the thinking from the work. This legacy lives on in the business world, where thinking is often discouraged while task completion is rewarded. Given the choice of a software program or a checklist or a spreadsheet that spits out an answer versus an opinion from a human brain, many businesses will opt for the nonbrain choice.

▷ How to think better

Changing our thinking is at the same time the hardest and the easiest thing to do. To that end, I have put together some exercises to help you think without a consultant. The point of these exercises is to help you think about your business in a different context, outside the management-method-fads context and into a creating-a-healthy-business-lifestyle paradigm. Keep in mind that these are not solutions, just ways to help you identify what might be a myth.

Thinking exercise 1: Strive to enhance humanity

If the basic building blocks of businesses are people, then anything that helps people improve should improve your business. The way I see it, organizations consist of four elements—the individuals, subgroups and their interactions, the entire group, and the interactions of the entire group with the rest of the world. This is a guideline I use to determine if a new program or initiative is going to help or harm the organization. It doesn't really matter what the initiative is called as long as it does one of the following:

1. Improve relationships. My biggest successes with process reengineering projects came when we improved relationships across different functional areas. Early initiatives in process reengineering and quality circles got people together to solve problems and share information. The biggest problem with talent management systems is that they replace relationships with paperwork and ratings. I have found that this is why some knowledge management efforts fail as well. They try to replace learning from someone else with a document. Whenever someone has extra budget money to spend on training, I usually recommend some kind of communications training. The more comfortable your organization is with open and honest conversations between all layers of the hierarchy, the more likely problems and issues will become visible quickly and resolved quickly. In my experience, many business problems are due to a lack of communication, and often my real value as a consultant is in being a communications vehicle between functions or levels. That's an expensive way to communicate.

If your program is going to improve relationships, you've got a winner. If it is an attempt to replace relationships, good luck with that!

2. Improve judgment or expand thinking. This could apply to anything that helps improve decision making and judgment, like better information, more insight, and clearer reports. Supply-chain automation delivered great benefits because all the suppliers and vendors could see the same information and make decisions based on it. Strategic planning is great at increasing knowledge. Metrics help, too. The problem is when you try to use these tools in place of judgment. A piece of paper or a complicated information system does not have the capacity for analysis, information gathering, synthesis, and conclusion that a human has. Automated call centers with push-button menus and standardized scripts are universally hated by customers because they try to replace human judgment. Databases with information on common problems and customer histories, however, help a customer service representative troubleshoot because they provide information to help judgment. There's a big difference between a checklist containing a list of questions to consider and one that calculates a rating at the bottom. People don't mind adding more questions to the former; it just gives them more to think about. However, if you have to tabulate every line item for a score, everyone will want to keep that checklist short and simple, thus providing less information to consider while making a decision.

Make sure your initiative is geared to improving the quality of thinking and not to finding a tool to replace thinking.

3. Create an environment that helps employees enjoy life. This would apply to initiatives like upgrading the office furniture, holding company picnics, and generally creating a fun place to work. I believe that anything a company does to improve the lives of the employees ultimately improves the relationships with the customers, the local community, and the corporate shareholders. As members of the human race, we have an obligation to each other to help make our lives worth living. As civilization

has advanced, we've mostly abolished practices like genocide and slavery. There is no reason to tolerate slavery in the workplace just because it has a salary attached. I have seen some dreadful places to work—mostly factories that were loud, dirty, polluted, unheated, and non-air-conditioned. Employees called in sick regularly and found every excuse to take a break. Wouldn't you? I have also seen factories that were clean, climate controlled, and noise controlled. Absenteeism wasn't a problem. Keeping costs low is no justification for treating employees like slaves, especially now in our stressed-out workplaces, where long hours, little vacation, and a working lunch are the norm. It doesn't even make good business sense. People need rest, exercise, and periodic breaks to think properly and be productive. I've been through several cost-cutting initiatives, and often some of the first things to be eliminated are the employee perks like free coffee, subsidized lunches, and discounted gym memberships. Only afterward do the cost cutters realize that these perks are all productivity enhancers.

More than enough data is available that shows investments in employees produce better company results, like growth in revenues and profits.

4. Strive to make life better for your customers. Although I think the best way to serve your customers well is to treat your employees well, I have heard enough anecdotes about companies that cheat their customers to warrant making this the fourth item on my list. I just don't see how you can create a sustainable business if the only goal is to make money for yourself. Isn't the point to create something valuable that you can charge money for? That's not the same as being in business to make money. We don't love Apple products because they have a high profit margin or buy pharmaceuticals because pharma companies have favorable earnings per share. We believe their products make our lives better, even in a small way. People tend to part with their money more

easily if they believe they are making their lives better with their purchase. From my experience, whenever a company changes the conversation from how to deliver better services to how to sell the most profitable engagements or from how to create lifesaving medicines to how to create hugely profitable medicines, it's been a warning sign that the company was embarking on a decline. I think of money as a measure—a measure of success. The money should be a means, not an end. When it becomes the end, a company is in danger of neglecting to add value, and that eventually means no more company.

If an initiative is geared to adding value to the world, then it has a much better chance of adding value to the company.

Thinking exercise 2: Use another context, or please try this at home

A common innovation thinking exercise is to alter the problem you are trying to solve by putting it in a different context. For instance, if you are trying to find ways to bring your products to market faster, you think of another context where you are trying to create something faster, like building a house or sculpting a piece of artwork. My thinking exercise 2 is to think about whether your program or initiative would be effective in a different aspect of life. If what you propose wouldn't work in another type of organization, it likely won't work in a business organization. Below are several (somewhat ridiculous) scenarios that take the subject matter of my chapters and apply it to other life situations.

Strategic plan development   Sara is an Ivy League graduate currently working at a prestigious consulting firm. The company is urging her to get her masters in business administration, but she is not sure what she wants to do with her life. The only consulting assignments she really enjoyed were in public policy. She decides to hire a team of life coaches to develop a five-year life plan for her. After interviewing Sara, her family, and her friends, they put together a plan: she should go to New York University law school and study international law. Afterward, she should join a prestigious global law firm, travel all over the world, fall in love with a partner and get married, and continue to work part-time in law while raising a family of one boy and one girl.

What happens if Sara gets offered a once-in-a-lifetime overseas consulting assignment with the World Bank? It will definitely derail her plan. Should she take it?

Process best practice implementation   You review your household finances and discover that your family is spending way more than they are taking in. This is a surprise because you earn a good salary and don't have lots of expenses. Clearly, someone is spending too much money! You decide your family needs a budget, so you look on the Internet and find a budgeting template to use. That night after dinner you show your family the template they will be required to use. After a month, you review the finances again and discover the problem is still there. While everyone had used the template, you notice that many expense entries are missing. So you decide to buy Quicken and install it on everyone's computer. Now every transaction will be recorded automatically. After a month, you review the Quicken reports and find you still have negative cash flows. You have tons of transactions to review in Quicken, but many of them seem to be miscategorized. You decide what you really need is a more robust software program and better enforcement of the process!

Target goals   Larry is the coach of a kids' soccer team. The team had a dismal record last year, so this year he decides to implement a few new policies to motivate the kids. After tryouts, Larry not only assigns the kids their positions, but also determines individual objectives for them—how many saves, goals scored, and defensive moves—dependent on position. There are per-game objectives and those for the entire season. Those kids that exceed their goals are rewarded with two scoops of ice cream after the game. Those that meet their goals get one scoop, while those that don't meet theirs get the pleasure of watching their teammates eat ice cream. What kind of team would this end up being?

Performance appraisal   You know, my kids are not really performing the way I think they should. This year I am going to review their behaviors and accomplishments in December and discuss all the things I think they should be doing better. To help them improve, I will rate them on academics, athletics, social leadership, and business acumen. My expectation is that they need a minimum competence in each of these areas to be successful in life. Their overall ratings will result in an adjustment to their allowance in the New Year. What kind of psychiatry bills are they going to incur later in life?

Performance coaching   While I'm trying to improve my kids, I should target my husband as well. He never does the dishes, and it drives me crazy. I took a weeklong class on relationship skills to address this issue, and now I have a feedback model to use on him: ASCA (Ask permission, be Specific, describe Consequences, create Actions). I tried the ASCA model, and he promised he would clean more often, but still nothing changed. After consulting with my feedback tip sheet, I realized that the actions weren't specific enough. Next, I developed an action plan outlining exactly when and how he needed to clean up and gave that to him. He rolled his eyes at me. Clearly he is uncoachable, and I need to file for divorce.

Poor-performance action plans   Unfortunately, Jan's career has caused her to move quite often, resulting in many school changes for her kids. Fortunately, Jan's children are quite intelligent and adaptable and usually adjust easily to their new schools, so their academic performance hasn't suffered. However, after this last move, Jan's oldest daughter is miserable, and her grades are terrible. She says it's because her new school is obsessed with football and cheerleading, two areas she has no interest in. This daughter complains that all her teachers use these sports in their classes as examples. Jan also suspects her daughter is being bullied because she doesn't attend any games. As a good parent, should Jan outline an action plan to get her daughter's grades up to passing before she looks for a different school?

Leadership assessments and development programs   I find the state of American politics quite distressing. Some of the candidates don't seem at all qualified to lead. Why doesn't politics take a cue from business? Before graduating from high school, every student should take a leadership assessment. Those people who score well should be picked to go to an Ivy League school to study law or public policy. This way, we can ensure we have a continuous supply of qualified candidates.

Last ridiculous scenario: consultant selection   You've been married for over a decade and have two small children. You and your spouse seem to be arguing over everything lately—finances, chores, lack of intimacy. After yet another argument last night, you began to cry uncontrollably, and the two of you finally started to talk about your problems. You both concluded that you still love each other very much, and you want to make it work, especially for the kids, but you need outside help. You decide to try marriage counseling. The two of you do research and ask for recommendations for a good counselor. You get five recommendations:

- Counselor 1 has a surefire five-step program to resolve all marital issues and will lead you through the program. The first step is on a website, so you can get started at home.

- Counselor 2 specializes in marital strife with young kids. She knows exactly what your problems are due to her work with other couples. She'll provide you with a manual outlining what to do and two consultation sessions if you have any questions on the material.

- Counselor 3 has a proprietary assessment for the two of you to take. Based on your results, he will formulate a custom solution based on his standard set of marital solutions.

- Counselor 4 is a famous author of several well-known books. She is also pricey and not readily available for counseling sessions. She recommends you buy her software program, which will lead you step-by-step through all the aspects of marriage counseling.

- Counselor 5 wants to sit and talk with the two of you about your problems and take it from there.

Which counselor do you choose?

Thinking exercise 3: Mean what you say and say what you mean

The root cause of many business problems is the conviction that business is something other than a group of people and that business issues and solutions are something other than what they really are. Much of this fallacious belief system is due to the way we talk. We all know business is full of obscure jargon, and I know that I have been guilty of relying on jargon in this book. Although we often joke about it, I don't think we spend enough time thinking about the consequences of the words we use (me, too). The words we use shape the way we think, which is why spin doctors are popular in politics. The easiest way to start changing how we think about business is by changing how we talk about business.

I am amused by the two overused phrases I hear in reaction to some of my ideas. When I explain why I think strategic plans are limiting, my colleagues often argue that I have it all wrong: "Strategic plans are supposed to be living documents." Living documents? Other than in Harry Potter movies, I've never seen a living document. And that's the problem. Rather than assigning resources to update the plan or putting a process in place to do so, management just dismisses all the work required to keep a strategic plan current with an "It's a living document." That's a complete abdication of responsibility in favor of reliance on magical paperwork. When I explain how numerical targets and incentive compensation encourage bad behavior, the reaction is, "How else do you hold people's feet to the fire?" Yikes! Why are we trying to torture our employees? The problem with torture is that you get exactly what you torture for, regardless of the truth, which is exactly what these systems do. We really need to pay attention to the language we use and start talking the truth rather than using euphemisms and aphorisms, or we will continually address symptoms rather than problems. "Creating efficiencies" means firing employees. "Restructuring" means firing even more employees. Unless we call things what they really are, we will never be able to fully understand them or respond appropriately.

Table 2 shows the topics I've discussed in the preceding chapters with alternatives for how we should describe them. Notice how the change of words changes what you think.

Table 2 **Translations of business jargon**

Business jargon	What it really is
Create a future vision—This sounds inspirational, right? Who wouldn't want to be part of a future vision?	Predict the future and try to make the prediction a reality. Well, now this sounds more dubious. I'm not sure I want to be a part of it.
Business process reengineering—This phrase evokes a disembodied chain of boxes with someone applying tools to fix it.	Improve the way people work— Oh, that's so different. We have to get together to talk about it.
SMART goals—For sure, I want my goals to be smart, not stupid.	Take the goal you want to achieve and change it to something else—Huh? Why would I want to do that?
Incentive compensation—I think I should "incent" my employees. (I love when these are referred to as "schemes.")	Manipulate people through the use of money—This sounds sleazy and makes me wary of the consequences.
Performance management system—I think I might need one of those.	Improve individual and team work—The only way to do this is by talking.
Poor performance—This warrants an individual performance plan.	Incompetence (or poor fit)—This person needs either training or a different job. I don't know what an action plan can do to help.
Leadership development— Definitely a must; we need a continuous pipeline of leaders.	Process to create a leader— How exactly does one do this? Does anyone really know?
Core competence—What the hell is a core competence?	Job skills—There are lots of these, too many for one person, and they need to be updated all the time.

The jargon phrases either warp or limit our thinking. When you call it what it really is, the problems become obvious. The other phrases we need to banish are "Manage the bottom line," "Maximize shareholder value," and anything similar. As in the weight-loss-versus-healthy-lifestyle analogy I used in chapter 3, we don't actually want to do these things. What we really want is to create and maintain a healthy company. Creating and maintaining a healthy company is completely different from playing around with numbers on a spreadsheet. A healthy company has to have a healthy organization full of healthy people with healthy relationships in a healthy environment.

This problem of using words to obfuscate what we really want is endemic throughout the business world, and we really need to stop. Many of my consulting colleagues hate the jargon as much as I do, but the blame lies squarely on the management consulting industry. We are the ones who coined the phrases. Much of the jargon can be traced back to a book or a method conceived or popularized by consultants. The crux of the problem is that consultants are expected to be thought leaders and are rated and compensated on thought leadership. What exactly is thought leadership? Thoughts are things we make up in our heads, and leadership is persuading everyone else to follow them. We've done a good job at that.

On behalf of all the management consultants everywhere who have filled your lives with meaningless jargon, delusional programs, and misleading models, I am truly and deeply sorry.

▷ How to think about working with consultants

None of this means that you should avoid hiring management consultants. In this age of very lean companies and outsourced workforces, it is almost impossible not to hire consultants. Using consultants has many benefits, especially on projects that are not part of normal operations. In my corporate career, there were as many times I wished we had hired outside expertise as there were times I wished the management consultants would disappear. Moreover, like hiring a personal trainer or a nutritionist, you tend to follow the advice when you have to pay for it. Sometimes, a company just needs the fresh perspective an outsider brings.

As a management consultant, I've occasionally found myself in lose-lose situations. Typically, this happens when clients have hidden agendas or are shirking their responsibilities. The worst thing a client can do is to hire someone to do their thinking for them. We can provide analyses, recommendations, expertise from other areas, and new ways of looking at situations, but the success and failure of the company needs to be with the leadership team, not the advisors. The other lose-lose situation I hate happens when clients don't trust the advice of their own people. As soon as I walk in the door, everyone resents me. Worse is when top executives don't like what their team is telling them so they hire consultants to buoy their own opinions. Remember, you can always find someone willing to say what you want to hear if you pay enough.

Table 3 sums up my advice on when consultants can benefit your organization and when they can't.

Table 3 **Reasons to hire a consultant**

Good reasons to hire a consultant	Questionable reasons to hire a consultant
The project is political and you need someone outside the corporate hierarchy to offer objective advice.	The project is work you really should be doing yourself, only you can't prioritize the workload so you bring in extra resources instead.
You could benefit from a different way of thinking.	You are really looking for an outside opinion to support your (unpopular) viewpoint.
Your company lacks specific expertise or experience.	You have hard decisions to make and decide to hire a consulting firm to make them for you.
You lack the resources needed to complete a project and need the extra help.	You really don't want to address this problem, but you are under pressure to resolve it so you offload it to consultants.
You could benefit from a project leader who can't get pulled off to work on other priorities and will see the project through to completion.	You are not ready to commit yourself to an initiative so you hope that someone else can just do it all for you without any company involvement.
The organization is not communicating well and someone needs to be a conduit across levels or silos.	The organization is dysfunctional and you want someone else to fix it.
Fresh bodies and ideas could invigorate a jaded organization.	You don't like any of the recommendations your internal staff have suggested because what you really want is that magic solution.

A successful consulting engagement is the result of a successful partnership. It really has to be a two-way relationship. In that respect, you need to find someone you are comfortable having a relationship with. Most of us consultants truly want to help our clients. This profession has its share of jerks, and I don't care how smart they are—you can't have a viable relationship with a jerk. However, many of the well-meaning consultants believe in all the mumbo jumbo they've created, and that's a problem, too. I know that I used to believe in the models and methods, especially proprietary ones. When they don't work, these consultants' advice is to do it again, only harder, because a step must have been missed or not executed well. You want a consultant who will listen, investigate, analyze, and probe before offering recommendations and solutions.

Here's my advice on what to look for and what to avoid when hiring consultants:

Table 4 **Advice for hiring a consultant**

Look for	Beware of
Someone who insists upon doing an up-front analysis before giving you any potential solutions.	Those offering one-size-fits all methodologies and solutions, especially those who don't do much of an up-front analysis.
Those who explain everything to you and outline their approach as well as what they will need from you.	People who speak in corporate mumbo jumbo. If they can't speak in plain English, either they don't know what they are doing or they don't want you to know what they are doing.

Continues on next page

Table 4 **Advice for hiring a consultant,** *continued*

Look for	Beware of
People who again insist on doing an analysis before they make any estimates of hard benefits. All their dollar benefits are clearly explained and usually contain an estimated range. All assumptions are clearly listed. Their estimates seem reasonable, not extravagant.	Those who promise huge benefits as soon as they walk in the door. Although this seems like a guarantee, beware of products and services that entice you to buy with a money-back guarantee. You don't know how they are going to keep their promises (like replacing experienced staff with entry-level hires).
People who have a breadth of experience and most certainly know how to do more than one thing. Having experience with your type of business isn't always necessary. Sometimes you need someone who understands your industry, but sometimes you could benefit from a different perspective. Overall, you need someone whose judgment you trust.	People with no real experience. Without experience, the only thing they can offer is a methodology. If the methodology isn't appropriate, they don't have the experience to recognize that.
People who genuinely listen to you and communicate honestly. When they don't know something, they tell you.	People who have an answer for everything and seem to always have exactly the experience you need. Likely, they are not being honest.
People you trust.	People you don't trust.

Conclusion

Several times, I've attempted to put together a list of what I have learned to create a tidy summary of the book. More than one person has asked me to do that. (If you really need the list, the chapter subheadings will do it for you.) Yet somehow I can't bring myself to do it. It's really very easy. I have an outline with all the points I wanted to make. All I have to do is "copy and paste." To be honest, I'm a little spooked by an early critique of this manuscript. One of the questions was whether I could be deemed an expert. While I think I'm pretty smart and knowledgeable (or is that the better-than-average effect?), that "expert" word bothers me. I'm not even sure what I am an expert in (common sense?). I don't want to write a list of lessons you should follow or summarize what you should do in bullet points because I'm not sure how much I want you to follow my lessons, and I certainly don't think you should take my recommendations at face value. I said at the beginning of the book that I don't want to contribute to the dogma. The only lesson I want you to take away from this book is that you should think about the consequences of a method or a best practice or a business solution before you embark on it. Just because other companies are doing it doesn't mean it's right.

That's the whole summary of this book. Don't believe the dogma and think about the consequences of what you are doing. I know that starting from a blank sheet of paper is scary. I think it's scary, too. But as long as you have a good team of people around you, which you likely do, you'll figure it out. People make the problems, and people can solve them, too. It's that obvious.

Notes
∇

Chapter 1

Characterization of the strategy consulting industry comes from the book by Walter Kiechel and book review by Garry Emmons of *The Lords of Strategy*, about the founders of the well-known strategy consulting firms.

The Boston Consulting Group had developed two famous quantitative models well before Porter's tools, the portfolio matrix model and the experience curve, which were both cash management tools. Porter's book added competition to the mix and offered the generic strategies.

The information on Jack Welch comes from a variety of web pages, including GE's corporate site, Encyclopedia.com, a *BusinessWeek* profile, and the *Economist*. The number of one hundred thousand layoffs is reported widely and can be justified from an *Economist* article on the Jack Welch MBA in 2009: "Mr. Welch earned the sobriquet Neutron Jack by analogy with the neutron bomb, which kills people but leaves buildings intact. GE had 411,000 workers at the end of 1980, just before he took charge, and 299,000 at the end of 1985. He also introduced the practice of firing each year the worst-performing 10% of GE's managers."

Blue Ocean Strategy, published in 2005, is a popular book on strategy that advocates being creative about constructing new market spaces rather than fighting in an existing landscape. Red oceans are a metaphor for bloody competitive battles, while blue oceans are open areas of opportunity that are as yet unexplored. This methodology also follows the "create a big, exciting vision and then create a plan around it" process.

In 1997, Clayton Christensen published a seminal book called *The Innovator's Dilemma*, which brought the phrase "disruptive innovation" into the business lexicon. The thesis of the book is that in their pursuit of a better market share and higher margins, companies tend to add more features to existing products and ignore creating the new innovations that will disrupt the existing products. This is because new innovations are typically unproven or unreliable and usually enter the market at a low price with low margins and no market share.

Chapter 2

Eliyahu Goldratt's theory of constraints was published in *The Goal: A Process of Ongoing Improvement.*

Information on the origins of Six Sigma was from a variety of website articles, including "The History of Six Sigma," and "The Evolution of Six Sigma," and from the book *The Six Sigma Way.* While it is undisputed that the movement started at Motorola, I have seen credit given to different engineers as the "father" of the movement, so I opted not to name names.

The origins of the fishbone diagram showing the reasons for a car not to start are not known by me. I started using that example at Gemini Consulting, and it was probably created by someone there.

Other versions of the fishbone with different categories are used for different industries and situations—for instance, using Ps (people, policies, procedures, processes, place). I chose the M (man, machine, materials, method, and milieu) version to show that even machine problems have people as their ultimate causes.

Chapter 3

The balanced scorecard article was "The Balanced Scorecard: Measures That Drive Performance" in *Harvard Business Review* by Robert S. Kaplan and David P. Norton. Since this article was published, they have written a few books and other articles on the balanced scorecard. Their first article is also reprinted periodically as an *HBR* classic.

The balanced scorecard in figure 2 is an example that I created for this book. It is loosely based on a real client example, but for confidentiality reasons I didn't want to use a real example. The same is true for the example of cascading key performance indicators in figure 3.

The first two metrics slides are from a presentation I used at Gemini. I was not the author, and I do not know who first created these.

The acronym "SMART" has many different definitions. The one I use is "specific, measurable, actionable, results-oriented, and time-bound." Usually, the definitions of *S* and *M* are consistent, while the *T* is some word with time in it. However, I have seen the *A* be a variety of words, including "achievable," "attainable," "agreed-upon," "assignable," and "appropriate" while the *R* can be "relevant" or "realistic" in addition to "results-oriented."

I am not sure who coined the acronym "SMART." While Peter Drucker has written about goal setting and is credited with management by objectives, he did not coin the term. Dr. George Doran claims to have originated the use of the acronym, but others have said it was in use before him. Also, some people use the acronym "SMARTER," with the *E* and *R* being used for some kind of evaluate/reevaluate step. I have yet to see the acronym "SMARTEST," so I'm going to claim it: *E* for "evaluate," *S* for "sign-off," and *T* for "throw-away." (My trademark application is pending.)

Many US companies are moving away from GAAP and adopting international financial reporting standards to conduct global business more seamlessly. However, to me this is just further evidence of the subjective nature of finance and accounting.

Chapter 4

A good overview of the above-average effect is "The Better-Than-Average Effect" by Mark D. Alicke and Olesya Govorun in the book *The Self in Social Judgment*.

In addition to Alfie Kohn's and Daniel Pink's popular works, other sources that show how monetary rewards can be harmful are

• Florian Ederer and Gustavo Manso's in "Is Pay-for-Performance Detrimental to Innovation?"

• Jeffrey Pfeffer's "Six Dangerous Myths About Pay" in the May–June 1998 edition of *HBR*

- Michael J. Cooper, Huseyin Gulen, and P. Raghavendra Rau's "Performance for Pay? The Relationship Between CEO Incentive Compensation and Future Stock Price Performance"

Plus, Teresa Amabile is doing research in how to best motivate your employees, and it's not money. Her book is *The Progress Principle*.

The Marc Hodak article is "Pay for Performance: Beating 'Best Practices,'" which appeared in *Chief Executive*, July/August 2006.

The book in which Peter Drucker outlined management by objectives is *The Practice of Management*, published in 1954. I haven't read this one.

Chapter 5

The book *First, Break All the Rules*, by Marcus Buckingham and Curt Coffman, cites Gallup research showing poor managers as a top reason people leave their jobs. *The Successful Manager's Handbook* is even longer these days. I have the sixth edition, published in 2000. A later edition was published in 2004.

Daniel Goleman's model was published in the March–April 2000 edition of *HBR* in an article entitled "Leadership That Gets Results."

I tend to rely on the *Harvard Business Review* because I have subscribed for years and because that is where most new theories on business management get published. Plus, it is much easier and cheaper to read an *HBR* article than to buy and read a whole book—even better because the journal includes synopses of the articles.

The *New York Times* article on Google was called "Google's Quest to Build a Better Boss," in March 2011.

Chapter 6

McKinsey consultants' laying the blame for the failure of their principles on Enron's implementation is from an article in the UK *Guardian Observer*, "The Firm That Built the House of Enron," March 23, 2002.

Jack Welch was famous for firing the bottom 10 percent at GE before *The War for Talent* was published.

My information on Einstein was drawn from a number of sources, including the Nobel Prize website biographies, Biography.com, Einstein.biz, Wikipedia (sorry), *Einstein, the Nobody*—a Nova documentary, *New York Times* articles and obituary, and a short biography by Antonio Moreno González.

My information on U. S. Grant was drawn from his personal memoirs, a biography by Jean Edward Smith called *Grant*, Biography.com, and *America's Civil War* magazine (online version), including an article called "Ulysses S. Grant's Lifelong Struggle with Alcohol."

The original study of the students was by Robert Rosenthal and Lenore Jacobson and was published in a 1968 article called "Pygmalion in the Classroom: Teacher Expectation and Pupils' Intellectual Development." They have a more recent book by the same name.

The labeling effect goes by other names, including "the Pygmalion effect" and "the Rosenthal effect," after the experiment above, as well as "stereotyping" and "self-fulfilling prophecy."

The paper about the Peter Principle is by Alessandro Pluchino, Andrea Rapisarda, and Cesare Garofalo and is called "The Peter Principle Revisited: A Computational Study," published in October 2009.

Einstein himself complained that mathematicians considered him to be a physicist and physicists considered him to be a mathematician. This statement was from an April 24, 2004, *New York Times* article called "From Companion's Lost Diary, A Portrait of Einstein in Old Age."

Chapter 7

I realize that the examples of good leaders are all male and mostly American. I wanted to choose well-known examples so readers would know something of the lives of the leaders I discuss. Because of the dominance of American culture, I am making the assumption that non-Americans may know something of the American leaders, while the reverse is less likely to be true.

Jefferson's dislike of public speaking is documented in various places, including "The Master of Monticello," a *New York Times* book review that includes an excerpt from *American Sphinx: The Character of Thomas Jefferson* by Joseph J. Ellis.

Information about the State of the Union messages is from the National Archives website. Jefferson's tradition of sending a report to Congress held for about a century until Woodrow Wilson addressed Congress in person.

Again, you can find Daniel Goleman's leadership traits in "Leadership That Gets Results."

The list of leaders with less-than-stellar people skills is subjective, and some may take issue with my choices. Mostly it is based on the press or lack of press these people have received over the course of my lifetime. Here are some of my reasons:

• *Larry Ellison*—His biography is *The Difference Between God and Larry Ellison: God Doesn't Think He's Larry Ellison.*

• *Carly Fiorina*—Two reasons are the glee with which the tech press reported her firing and her comments about Barbara Boxer during her senatorial campaign.

• *Meg Whitman*—The press has reported on her volatile temper, and her abrasive manner was apparent during her gubernatorial campaign.

• *Jack Welch*—He seems to work hard to keep himself in the spotlight, his perks from GE after his retirement were quite a surprise, and anyone who insists on firing the bottom 10 percent is problematic in my book.

• *Michael Eisner*—He had well-publicized feuds with Jeffrey Katzenberg and Michael Ovitz, among others.

Whitman, Fiorina, and Eisner are all cited in the *Forbes* "Seven Habits of Spectacularly Unsuccessful CEOs Hall of Shame," February 9, 2012, for bad personal behavior.

Sam Walton, Lou Gerstner, Warren Buffett, Herb Kelleher, and Walt Disney are usually reported to be nice guys and lack the negative press that CEOs often receive.

Information about Steve Jobs was from Walter Isaacson's "The Genius of Jobs," published in the *New York Times* on October 30, 2011, and also his best-selling biography, *Steve Jobs*. Other sources were an interview with *60 Minutes*, a short biography by Romain Moisescot, and websites including the Apple Museum (applemuseum.bott.org).

The information about Manfred Kets de Vries was from a January 2004 article in *Harvard Business Review* called "Putting Leaders on the Couch: A Conversation with Manfred F. R. Kets de Vries," as well as his official website, http://www.ketsdevries.com.

The information about Michael Maccoby was from a January 2004 article in *Harvard Business Review* called "Narcissistic Leaders: The Incredible Pros, the Inevitable Cons." He also has a book called *Narcissistic Leaders: Who Succeeds and Who Fails* (2007), but I haven't read it.

Chapter 8

The information on Frederick Taylor is from Taylor's *Principles of Scientific Management* and Stewart's *The Management Myth*, as well as a couple of articles from websites with biographical information: "Frederick Taylor and Scientific Management" (http://www.netmba .com/mgmt/scientific/) and "Frederick Winslow Taylor" (http://www .eldritchpress.org/fwt/taylor.html).

Champy and Hammer mention in their book *Reengineering the Corporation* that 50–70 percent of reengineering efforts fail. They blame a lack of knowledge and ability for this failure rate and categorize reengineering efforts as high risk.

A variety of sources cite high failure rates for mergers and acquisitions. "The Big Idea: The New M&A Playbook" at the *Harvard Business Review* website (http://hbr.org/2011/03/the-big-idea-the -new-ma-playbook/ar/1) cites 70–90 percent failure rate.

The incentive compensation failure is from Hodak's and Cooper, Gulen, and Rau's studies.

The rest of the chapter is my advice.

Resource A: A Measure of Truth
▽

You didn't expect to read a book by a management consultant and not have some sort of scorecard, did you? I thought I would summarize what I know to be true about conventional management wisdom based on my decades-long career, which includes reading tons of business books and research. I have to put a disclaimer on the accuracy of this information because I can't be expected to be familiar with all the research in all these areas, but I am putting a stake in the ground in the hopes that this will become a living document. Oops, I slipped. Sorry about that; old habits die hard. Let me rephrase: you can find this scorecard on the web at imsorryibrokeyourcompany.com and add any research or other theories you think should be included.

The Truthometer

Theory	Truth Index	Sources
Pay-for-performance or incentive compensation motivates and aligns employees to the company objectives.	False	Daniel Pink, Marc Hodak, Alfie Kohn; Florian Ederer and Gustavo Manso; Jeffrey Pfeffer; Michael J. Cooper, Huseyin Gulen, and P. Raghavendra Rau

Continues on next page

The Truthometer, *continued*

Theory	Truth Index	Sources
Goals with numerical targets or metrics motivate employees to perform better.	False	Jeffrey Pfeffer; Gregg Stocker, Lisa Ordóñez, Maurice Schweitzer, Adam Galinsky, and Max H. Baze ("Goals Gone Wild"); Michael Jensen
Annual performance appraisals, especially those with ratings, help improve employee performance.	False	Tom Coens and Mary Jenkins, Sam Culbert, Troy Grubb
Companies need a good strategy to be successful.	Unproven	Lots of papers have been written on how to create strategies but none that shows you need one.
Leadership requires mastery of certain traits.	Unproven	Lots of studies link leadership ability with specific traits, but no real consensus has been reached on the traits, except for some kind of drive or motivation.
Good people management requires good people skills.	True	Aside from Google's Project Oxygen, not a lot of data exists, but this seems like a reasonable assumption. Also, there is no contrary evidence.
Companies that invest in their employees tend to outperform those that don't. (Investment in training, other development, and morale-boosting activities.)	True	Human Capital Institute, Great Places to Work, ASTD, Workplace Research Foundation, Gallup, Workforce.com

Resource B: The Method of Truth
▽

Although management is not a science, we can still learn from science. In fact, I love science, and I love learning from it. What science can most offer to businesses is not theories but the method in which science is conducted. The purpose of science is to derive the truth. Physics seeks to find the underlying laws governing the physical world, from atomic particles to the origins of the universe. Biology seeks to understand life. Chemistry seeks to understand how molecules interact. Science is not about creating a set of laws; it's about understanding how things work and changing the laws based on new information. Many people seem to confuse ideologies with scientific theories. Theories change, while ideologies do not. Astrology and creationism are not science. They are static belief systems that don't seek to find underlying truths. They try to bend theories to conform to the beliefs. Our current state of management "science" also doesn't seem to be very interested in finding the truth.

Although I have spent most of this book debunking popular methodologies, one proven method should be used much more often in businesses, a method that could be used to derive the truth about how people work—the scientific method.

Scientific method

Usually the scientific method is written as four steps, but sometimes people break the four steps down into finer detail with six or seven resulting steps. I'm going with the four-step approach I was taught in grade school.

1. Research, analyze, investigate, and define the problem

I don't know if this is symptomatic of the American culture, but we are so action oriented and impatient to get to the solutions that we spend very little time understanding the problem. The first step of the scientific method is to define the problem, and to define the problem, you need to understand it. How you define the problem sets the course of all the following actions. Finding the root causes of problems and fixing those can save countless hours and money compared to constantly addressing the symptoms of problems. This habit of addressing symptoms always results in new symptoms that need fixing. Spending a little time finding out the "why" before moving on to the "how" can save time in the long run.

Several years ago, I was asked to participate in a cross-functional, problem-solving session to brainstorm ideas on how to get more employees involved in community volunteer activities. The session came up with some very creative public relations ideas and actions to take. However, no one spent any time researching why employees weren't getting involved. Instead, according to the consultant's advice to phrase problems in a "how to" format to solicit actions, we worked on the wrong problem. The real issue was that employees equated involvement in these activities with being a low-level or unimportant employee. In addition, many employees thought that these activities were meant to provide leadership opportunities for the administrative staff. Our list of brainstorming ideas and actions didn't try to change that perception. All we had to do to solve the problem was to get some senior management involved in these activities.

2. Develop hypotheses based on the research

My experience with human-caused problems is that often you'll find the cause of the problem in the first step, so this one isn't often needed. However, when you can't easily find the solution, developing hypotheses helps expand your thinking. Notice that this step involves multiple hypotheses based on your research, not just one. The problem with our thinking is that we like to narrow down our options too early and adopt an initial solution just because it is the first one that might work. Then, once we've adopted it as the solution, we are unlikely to change our minds even with new information. If you formulate multiple hypotheses, you expand your search and have a higher probability of finding the correct option than if you narrow down your solutions early on.

3. Experiment and test the hypotheses

In new product development, the key to success is fast failure, not early perfection. The point is to figure out as quickly as possible all the product features that don't work and eliminate those from further inquiry. Management theorists need to adopt the habit of eliminating unsound theories. Instead, each model and method adds to the body of knowledge, and businesses try to implement everything. Worse, one clever consultant finds a new way of combining unrelated ideas and then other consultants build on it until it becomes a mishmash of conceptual frameworks. No manner of adjustment is ever going to get a faulty assumption to work right. Scientists know that when a hypothesis doesn't work, they need to move on to the next one.

4. Discern findings, formulate conclusions, and repeat step 3

Most often, this step is written as just "formulate conclusions." I have separated out findings from conclusions because I have found that many businesspeople don't understand the difference. The scientific method is an iterative process; it is unlikely that one experiment will provide enough evidence to allow you to draw conclusions. Rather, it should provide information, aka findings, on where to investigate further. This point is becoming more important because the ability to survey large groups of people and perform a variety of data analyses on the information gathered has become infinitely easier in the last decade. However, people frequently misinterpret the data and see conclusions where none exist. The term "highly correlated" is bandied about as if it means two data points have an irrefutable cause-and-effect relationship, but two data points could be highly correlated due to a number of inconclusive reasons.

For example, one stock market predictor is the Super Bowl Index (SBI). The SBI states that the stock market will rise in years in which the NFC (National Football Conference) team wins the Super Bowl, and it has an 80 percent correlation. Statistically, that's a very high correlation, so make sure you buy stocks whenever the NFC wins! However, when you examine the SBI more closely, you realize that there is no relationship between the variables at all. The NFC teams win the Super Bowl more often than the AFC (American Football Conference), and the stock market has more bull years (it goes up over time) than bear years. Any randomly chosen year should see a bull market and an NFC win. The two highly correlated variables have no actual relationship to each other.

Not too long ago, I had a phone conversation with a representative from a large talent management consultancy on its menu of leadership assessments. The woman assured me that using her firm's leadership assessments was highly correlated with business success. When I asked her to explain this, she said that statistical analyses showed that clients who used these assessments performed above the industry average in revenue growth.

Therefore, using these assessments would make a company successful, at least in terms of revenue growth. However, a much more plausible explanation is that successful companies, those with money, are more likely to buy leadership assessments than those without money. Another more plausible hypothesis is that companies that invest in employee development are likely to outperform those that don't. Making the conclusion that company success was due to the use of leadership assessments is more a leap of faith than an evidence-based result. The only conclusion you can reach from two highly correlated variables is that you need to do more research.

Resource C: Bibliography

▽

Akpose, Wole. "A History of Six Sigma." *IEEE-US Today's Engineer*. December 2010. http://www.todaysengineer.org/2010/Dec/six -sigma.asp.

Alicke, Mark, and Oleysa Govorun. "The Better-Than-Average Effect." In *The Self in Social Judgment*, edited by Mark Alicke, David Dunning, and Joachim Krueger, 94–116. New York: Psychology Press, 2005.

Alter, Adam. "Why It's Dangerous to Label People." *Psychology Today*. May 17, 2010. http://www.psychologytoday.com/blog/alterna tive-truths/201005/why-its-dangerous-label-people.

Amabile, Teresa and Steven Kramer. *The Progress Principle: Using Small Wins to Ignite Joy, Engagement, and Creativity at Work*. Boston: Harvard Business Review Press, 2011.

Bassi, Laurie J., and Daniel P. McMurrer. "Investing in Companies That Invest in People." Bassi Investments. January 2002. http://www .bassi-investments.com/downloads/Article_hr.com.pdf.

Bennis, Warren. *On Becoming a Leader*. Reading, MA: Addison-Wesley, 1989.

Bercovici, Jeff. "Why (Some) Psychopaths Make Great CEOs." *Forbes*. June 14, 2011. http://www.forbes.com/sites/jeffbercovici/2011 /06/14/why-some-psychopaths-make-great-ceos/.

Blanchard, Ken, Patricia Zigarmi, and Drea Zigarmi. *Leadership and the One Minute Manager*. New York: William Morrow, 1985.

Biography.com. "Albert Einstein Biography." Accessed April 14, 2012. http://www.biography.com/people/albert-einstein-9285408.

———. "Ulysses S. Grant Biography." Accessed April 14, 2012. http:// www.biography.com/people/ulysses-s-grant-9318285.

Bodanis, David. "Einstein the Nobody." Nova. October 11, 2005. http:// www.pbs.org/wgbh/nova/physics/einstein-the-nobody.html/.

Borjas, Thomas. "Welch, Jack, 1935–." *International Directory of Business Biographies*. 2005. Encyclopedia.com. http://www.encyclopedia.com /topic/Jack_Welch.aspx.

Bryant, Adam. "Google's Quest to Build a Better Boss." *New York Times*. March 13, 2011, BU1.

Byrne, John A. "How Jack Welch Runs GE." *BusinessWeek*. June 6, 1998. http://www.businessweek.com/1998/23/b3581001.htm.

———. "Inside McKinsey." *BusinessWeek*. July 8, 2002. http://www .businessweek.com/magazine/content/02_27/b3790001.htm.

Businessballs.com. "Six Sigma." Accessed April 14, 2012. http://www .businessballs.com/sixsigma.htm.

Champy, James, and Michael Hammer. *Reengineering the Corporation*. New York: Harper Collins, 2001.

Christensen, Clayton M. *The Innovator's Dilemma*. New York: Harper Business, 2000.

Christensen, Clayton, Richard Alton, Curtis Rising, and Andrew Waldeck. "The New M&A Playbook." *Harvard Business Review*. March 2011. http://hbr.org/2011/03/the-big-idea-the-new-ma -playbook/ar/1.

Coens, Tom, and Mary Jenkins. *Abolishing Performance Appraisals*. San Francisco: Berrett-Koehler, 2000.

Cohen, Shoshanah, and Joseph Roussel. *Strategic Supply Chain Management*. New York: McGraw-Hill, 2005.

Collins, James, and Jerry Porras. "Building Your Company's Vision." *Harvard Business Review*. September 1996. http://hbr.org/1996/09 /building-your-companys-vision/ar/1.

Collins, Jim. *Good to Great*. New York: HarperCollins, 2001.

Cooper, Michael J., Huseyin Gulen, and P. Raghavendra Rau. "Performance for Pay? The Relationship Between CEO Incentive Compensation and Future Stock Price Performance." *Wall Street Journal*. December 2009. http://online.wsj.com/public/resources /documents/CEOperformance122509.pdf.

Coutu, Diane L. "Putting Leaders on the Couch: A Conversation with Manfred F. R. Kets de Vries." *Harvard Business Review*. January 2004, 64–71.

Covey, Stephen R. *The 7 Habits of Highly Effective People*. New York: Fireside, 1989.

Craighead, Jon. "A Brief History of Business Strategy Consulting." June 2011. http://www.craigheadassociates.com/History_of_Strategy _Consulting.pdf.

Creveling, Clyde, Lynne Hambleton, and Burke McCarthy. *Six Sigma for Marketing Processes.* Upper Saddle River, NJ: Prentice Hall, 2006.

Culbert, Samuel. *Get Rid of the Performance Review.* New York: Business Plus, 2010.

Dodd, Dominic, and Ken Favarro. "Managing the Right Tension." *Harvard Business Review.* December 2006, 15.

Economist. "The House That Jack Built." September 16, 1999. http:// www.economist.com/node/239557.

————. "The Jack Welch MBA." June 23, 2009. http://www.economist .com/node/13892633.

Ederer, Florian, and Gustavo Manso. "Is Pay-for-Performance Detrimental to Innovation?" Working paper, Haas School of Business, University of California, Berkeley. July 14, 2012. http:// faculty.haas.berkeley.edu/manso/em.pdf.

Eldritch Press. "Frederick Winslow Taylor." Accessed May 27, 2012. http://www.eldritchpress.org/fwt/taylor.html.

Elmerraji, Jonas. "Debunking the Super Bowl Indicator." *Penny Sleuth.* February 6, 2012. http://pennysleuth.com/debunking-the-super -bowl-indicator/.

Emmons, Garry. "The Lords of Strategy." *HBS Alumni Bulletin.* March 2010. http://www.alumni.hbs.edu/bulletin/2010/march/strategy.html.

Fisher, Lawrence M. "Sears Auto Centers Halt Commissions After Flap." *New York Times.* June 23, 1992. http://www.nytimes.com/1992/06 /23/business/sears-auto-centers-halt-commissions-after-flap.html.

Gardner, John W. *On Leadership.* New York: Free Press, 1990.

GE. "Past Leaders: John F. Welch, Jr." Accessed March 12, 2012. http://www.ge.com/company/history/bios/john_welch.html.

Gebelein, Susan, Lisa Stevens, Carol Skube, David Lee, Brian Davis, and Lowell Hellervik. *Successful Manager's Handbook.* Minneapolis: Personnel Decisions International, 1992.

George, Michael, David Rowlands, Mark Price, and John Maxey. *Lean Six Sigma Pocket Toolbook.* New York: McGraw-Hill, 2005.

Gladwell, Malcolm. "The Talent Myth." *New Yorker.* July 22, 2002. http:// www.newyorker.com/archive/2002/07/22/020722fa_fact?current Page=all.

Goldratt, Eliyahu. *The Goal: A Process of Ongoing Improvement.* Great Barrington, MA: North River Press, 1992.

Goleman, Daniel. "Leadership That Gets Results." *Harvard Business Review.* March–April 2000, 78–90.

González, Antonio Moreno. "Albert Einstein." Donostia International Physics Center. Accessed June 14, 2012. http://dipc.ehu.es/digitalak /pdf/ingelesa.pdf.

Grant, Ulysses S. *The Complete Personal Memoirs of Ulysses S. Grant.* New York: Modern Library, 1999.

Grubb, Troy. "Performance Appraisal Reappraised: It's Not All Positive." *Journal of Human Resource Education* 1, no. 1 (Summer 2007): 1–22.

Guardian Observer. "The Firm That Built the House of Enron." March 23, 2002. http://www.guardian.co.uk/business/2002/mar/24/enron .theobserver.

Hamel, Gary, and C. K. Prahalad. *Competing for the Future.* Boston: Harvard Business School Press, 1994.

———. "The Core Competence of the Corporation." *Harvard Business Review OnPoint,* May–June 1990, 1–15.

Hautala, Tiina M. "Leaders' Personality and Its Impact on the Subordinates' Expectations of Leadership." Paper presented at Psychological Type and Culture—East & West: A Multicultural Research Conference. Honolulu, HI, January 2006.

HistoryNet.com. "Ulysses S. Grant's Lifelong Struggle with Alcohol." *America's Civil War,* June 12, 2006. http://www.historynet.com /ulysses-s-grants-lifelong-struggle-with-alcohol.htm.

Hodak, Marc. "Pay for Performance: Beating 'Best Practices.'" *Chief Executive,* July/August 2006.

Isaacson, Walter. *Steve Jobs.* New York: Simon & Schuster, 2011.

———. "The Genius of Jobs." *New York Times.* October 30, 2011, SR1–8.

Jackson, Eric. "The Seven Habits of Spectacularly Unsuccessful CEOs Hall of Shame." *Forbes.* February 9, 2012. http://www.forbes.com /sites/ericjackson/2012/02/09/the-seven-habits-of-spectacularly -unsuccessful-ceos-hall-of-shame/.

Jensen, Michael. "Paying People to Lie: The Truth About the Budgeting Process." *European Financial Management.* 2003, 379–406.

Jobs, Steve. Interview by Dan Rather on *60 Minutes. CBS News.* Released March 4, 2009.

Kaplan, Robert S., and David P. Norton. "The Balanced Scorecard: Measures That Drive Performance." *Harvard Business Review.* January–February 1992.

Kaplan, Steven E., Michael J. Petersen, and Janet A. Samuels. "Effects of Subordinate Likeability and Balanced Scorecard Format on Performance-Related Judgments." Paper presented at the Management Accounting Section Midyear Meeting, Fort Worth, TX, January 2007. http://aaahq.org/mas/MASPAPERS2007 /balanced.scorecards/Kaplan%20Petersen%20and%20Samuels.pdf.

Kets de Vries. "Manfred Kets de Vries." Accessed June 6, 2012. http:// www.ketsdevries.com.

Kiechel, Walter. *The Lords of Strategy: The Secret Intellectual History of the New Corporate World.* Boston: Harvard Business School Press, 2010.

Kim, W. Chan, and Renée Mauborgne. *Blue Ocean Strategy.* Boston: Harvard Business School Press, 2005.

———. "Blue Ocean Strategy." *Harvard Business Review*, October 2004, 76–84.

Knowledge at Wharton. "There's Just One Word for Jack Welch . . ." September 13, 2001. http://knowledge.wharton.upenn.edu/article .cfm?articleid=423.

Kohn, Alfie. *Punished by Rewards: The Trouble with Gold Stars, Incentive Plans, A's, Praise, and Other Bribes.* Boston: Houghton Mifflin, 1999.

Kotter, John P. "What Leaders Really Do." *Harvard Business Review.* December 2001.

Lepore, Jill. "Not So Fast: The History of Management Consulting." *New Yorker.* October 12, 2009. http://www.newyorker.com/arts /critics/atlarge/2009/10/12/091012crat_atlarge_lepore.

Linden, David J. "Addictive Personality? You Might Be a Leader." *New York Times.* July 24, 2011, SR4.

Maccoby, Michael. "Narcissistic Leaders: The Incredible Pros, the Inevitable Cons." *Harvard Business Review.* January 2004, 92–101.

May, Gary, and Lisa Gueldenzoph. "The Impact of Social Style on Student Peer Evaluation Ratings in Group Projects." Paper presented at the Association for Business Communication Annual Convention, Albuquerque, NM, October 2003.

Mayo Clinic staff. "Narcissistic Personality Disorder." Mayo Clinic. November 4, 2011. http://www.mayoclinic.com/health/narcissistic -personality-disorder/DS00652.

McKay, Matthew, Patrick Fanning, and Kim Paleg. *Couple Skills: Making Your Relationship Work.* Oakland, CA: New Harbinger, 2006.

Mesa, Andy. "Introduction." The Apple Museum. Accessed June 17, 2012. http://applemuseum.bott.org/.

Michaels, Ed, Helen Hanfield-Jones, and Beth Axelrod. *The War for Talent.* Boston: Harvard Business School Press, 2001.

Mintzberg, Henry, Bruce Ahlstrand, and Joseph Lampel. *Strategy Safari.* New York: Free Press, 1998.

Moisescot, Romain. "Long Bio." AllaboutSteveJobs.com. 2010. http://allaboutstevejobs.com/bio/longbio.php.

Murphy, Kevin R., Jeanette N. Cleveland, Amie L. Skattebo, and Ted B. Kinney. "Raters Who Pursue Different Goals Give Different Ratings." *Journal of Applied Psychology* 89, no. 1 (2004): 158–164.

NetMBA. "Frederick Taylor and Scientific Management." Accessed May 27, 2012. http://www.netmba.com/mgmt/scientific/.

New York Times. "Dr. Albert Einstein Dies in Sleep at 76; World Mourns Loss of Great Scientist." On This Day. April 19, 1955. http://www.nytimes.com/learning/general/onthisday/bday/0314.html.

Nobelprize.org. "Albert Einstein—Biography." Accessed April 15, 2012. http://www.nobelprize.org/nobel_prizes/physics/laureates/1921/einstein-bio.html.

Ordóñez, Lisa D., Maurice E. Schweitzer, Adam D. Galinsky, and Max H. Baze. "Goals Gone Wild: The Systematic Side Effects of Over-Prescribing Goal Setting." Working Paper 09-083, Harvard Business School, 2009.

Overbye, Dennis. "From Companion's Lost Diary, A Portrait of Einstein in Old Age." *New York Times.* April 24, 2004. http://www.nytimes.com/2004/04/24/nyregion/from-companion-s-lost-diary-a-portrait-of-einstein-in-old-age.html?pagewanted=all&src=pm.

Pande, Peter S., Robert P. Neuman, and Roland R. Cavanagh. *The Six Sigma Way: How GE, Motorola, and Other Top Companies Are Honing Their Performance.* New York: McGraw-Hill, 2000.

Peter, Lawrence, and Raymond Hull. *The Peter Principle.* Cutchogue, NY: Buccaneer Books, 1969.

Pfeffer, Jeffrey. "Six Dangerous Myths About Pay." *Harvard Business Review,* May–June 1998, 109–119.

Pink, Daniel. *Drive: The Surprising Truth About What Motivates Us.* New York: Riverhead Books, 2009.

Pluchino, Alessandro, Andrea Rapisarda, and Cesare Garofalo. "The Peter Principle Revisited: A Computational Study." Preprint submitted to Elsevier Science, October 29, 2009.

Pohl, Rüdiger F. "Effects of Labelling." In *Cognitive Illusions*, edited by Rüdiger F. Pohl, 327–344. New York: Psychology Press, 2004.

Porter, Michael. *Competitive Strategy: Techniques for Analyzing Industries and Competitors.* New York: Free Press, 1980.

Prentice, W. C. H. "Understanding Leadership." *Harvard Business Review*, January 2004, 102–109.

Process Quality Associates. "The Evolution of Six Sigma." Accessed April 14, 2012. http://www.pqa.net/ProdServices/sixsigma/W06002009.html.

Rosenthal, Robert, and Lenore Jacobson. *The Pygmalion Effect.* Norwalk, CT: Crown House, 1992.

Rosenthal, Robert, and Lenore Jacobson. "Pygmalion in the Classroom: Teacher Expectation and Pupils' Intellectual Development." In *The Production of Reality: Essays and Readings in Social Interaction.* 2nd ed. Edited by Jodi O'Brien and Peter Kollock, 443–447. Thousand Oaks, CA: Pine Forge Press, 1997.

Schoorman, David. "Escalation Bias in Performance Appraisals." *Journal of Applied Psychology* 73, no. 1 (1988): 58–62.

Schwartz, Nelson D., and J. B. Silver-Greenberg. "Bank Officials Cited in Churn of Foreclosures." *New York Times.* March 12, 2012. http://www.nytimes.com/2012/03/13/business/federal-report-cites-bank-officials-in-foreclosure-surge.html?_r=3&scp=1&sq=mortgage%20foreclosure%20federal%20report&st=cse.

Shweta. "Top Reasons for Poor Performance at Work." CareerBright. Accessed April 14, 2012. http://careerbright.com/career-self-help/top-reasons-for-poor-performance-at-work.

Smith, Jean Edward. *Grant.* New York: Touchstone, 2001.

Staples, Brent. "The Master of Monticello." *New York Times.* March 23, 1997. http://www.nytimes.com/books/97/03/23reviews/970323.23staplet.html.

Stewart, Matthew. *The Management Myth: Why the Experts Keep Getting It Wrong.* New York: W. W. Norton, 2009.

Stocker, Gregg. "Avoiding the Corporate Death Spiral." Speech given at CCPortugal, Sintra, Portugal, May 2009.

Tannenbaum, Robert, and Warren H. Schmidt. "How to Choose a Leadership Pattern." *Harvard Business Review* 36 (March–April 1958): 95–101.

Taylor, Frederick Winslow. *The Principles of Scientific Management.* Project Gutenberg, 2002. First published 1911. http://www.guten berg.org/files/6435/6435.txt.

Top Documentary Films. *A Class Divided.* Accessed April 14, 2012. http://topdocumentaryfilms.com/a-class-divided/.

Ward, David, and Elena Rivani. "An Overview of Strategy Development Models and the Ward-Rivani Model." *Econ Papers Archive.* June 7, 2005. http://129.3.20.41/econ-wp/get/papers/0506/0506002.pdf.

Wikipedia. "Albert Einstein." Last modified July 29, 2012. http://en.wikipedia.org/wiki/Albert_Einstein.

———. "Jack Welch." Last modified July 24, 2012. http://en.wikipedia.org/wiki/Jack_Welch.

———. "Scientific Management." Last modified May 20, 2012. http://en.wikipedia.org/wiki/Scientific_management.

Acknowledgments
▽

Mostly, I want to thank the people who have helped me bring this book to fruition. My main supporter and most reliable critic was my husband, Tom Hennigan, who gave me the best advice and also tolerated my moods. In that vein, I should also thank my children, Aidan and Alex, for putting up with my crankiness. Like some people discover they are mean drunks, I have discovered that I am a grumpy writer.

I'd like to thank Mark Hurwich for his eagerness to help me no matter what the endeavor and for his always spot-on critiques. Without him, this book would never have happened. I also want to thank Rich Catanese for his feedback and his encouragement. My business partners are also due some thanks: Peg MacBeth for her kind words of support and Dwight Ueda for putting up with my delayed deadlines while I worked on the manuscript. My friend Julie Ruth supplied me with wise and practical advice on more than one occasion and continues to be my best sounding board.

This book wouldn't be possible without the wonderful folks at Berrett-Koehler. They provided me with a great community of resources and a supportive environment. Some of the people at BK and its associates who were invaluable were Neal Maillet, Jeevan Sivasubramaniam, Michael Crowley, Katie Sheehan, Dianne Platner, Richard Wilson, Sharon Goldinger, and Beverly Butterfield. I apologize to anyone I may have inadvertently left out.

I'd also like to thank those reviewers that BK rounded up for all their helpful feedback, including Katherine Armstrong, Tora Estep, Pamela Gordon, and Wally Bock.

Index

▽

About the Author
▽

Karen Phelan was born the daughter of poor, Southern sharecroppers and as a child educated herself by reading *Pilgrim's Progress* by candlelight in her family's log cabin. Oops, that's totally not true. Karen's parents were middle-class, Irish immigrants who resided in a Cape Cod home on the outskirts of New York City. As a child, she strongly suspected that she was adopted. However, as a grown woman, she finds herself doing all the things her mother did that drove her crazy, and the shared gene pool has become evident. This turns out to be advantageous as the sheer amount of her Irish relatives could put this book on the best-seller list.

Karen suffered through twelve years of parochial school, but despite the good nuns' best efforts, they were not able to beat the sass out of her. However, they did successfully beat good grammar and spelling into her, which proved quite useful in later years. Afterward, Karen went to MIT, where she studied materials science and engineering and learned how to manipulate metals and ceramics at the atomic level. At MIT, she made the most important discovery of her career—she was, indeed, a nerd. As part of an MIT masters program (did she mention she went to MIT?), she worked in a military research facility in Los Angeles. While there, she did not get caught in a mantrap door or get her head stuck in the security gate like many of her colleagues, and thus she concluded that she wasn't cut out for government work. Instead, she decided to pursue a lifelong ambition to travel, so she joined the management consulting practice of Deloitte Haskins & Sells (now Deloitte & Touche). There she specialized in supply chain and manufacturing and traveled to all the glamorous hotbeds of American industry. Eventually, she joined Gemini Consulting, where she switched her career focus to process reengineering, change management, and training, but continued to travel to scenic manufacturing sites. She learned many useful lessons during this time, first and foremost that her college degrees had no practical applications outside her field. However, other lessons stayed with her for life, and to this day she knows her way around most US airports, the big hotel chains, and fast-food menus.

Seeking a more stable and settled lifestyle after starting a family, Karen joined Pfizer Consumer Healthcare. First, she managed a training group, but then she took on an international IT management role and found herself traveling again. (So much for settled!) While at Pfizer, she also worked on acquisitions and divestitures, including her own, when her division was bought by Johnson & Johnson. (So much for stability!) Next, she took an online marketing position at the J&J division that was later investigated by the FDA. She realized she was poorly suited to marketing when she pondered daily why anyone would need so many personal care products or want to have a relationship with a brand.

In 2008, she left J&J to help start a US office for an Australian software company that was relying on venture capital for its expansion. Several months later, the US financial crisis hit, funding was denied, and she decided that she didn't want to work for free. Now Karen has found her passion and is back working as a management consultant, this time as a cofounder of Operating Principals. Operating Principals is on a mission to help companies replace onerous human resource practices and systems with better dialogue, better relationships, and better employee job fit. Its operating principle is that simple acts often have the most profound results, and many workplaces are rife with needless complexity and bureaucracy.

Karen has been married to Tom Hennigan for twenty-two years and has learned that the secret to a long-lasting marriage is neither love nor commitment but rather inertia. She is mom to two teenage boys, Aidan and Alex, who currently wish they were adopted. (Sorry, boys!) They reside in an idyllic lake community in northern New Jersey (yes, New Jersey), nestled between Greenwood Lake and a state forest, living at one with nature. In other words, the bears regularly raid the trash, the raccoons have the run of the garage, and the chipmunks enjoy digging up the garden.

![BK logo] Berrett–Koehler
Publishers

Berrett-Koehler is an independent publisher dedicated to an ambitious mission: *Creating a World That Works for All*.

We believe that to truly create a better world, action is needed at all levels—individual, organizational, and societal. At the individual level, our publications help people align their lives with their values and with their aspirations for a better world. At the organizational level, our publications promote progressive leadership and management practices, socially responsible approaches to business, and humane and effective organizations. At the societal level, our publications advance social and economic justice, shared prosperity, sustainability, and new solutions to national and global issues.

A major theme of our publications is "Opening Up New Space." Berrett-Koehler titles challenge conventional thinking, introduce new ideas, and foster positive change. Their common quest is changing the underlying beliefs, mindsets, institutions, and structures that keep generating the same cycles of problems, no matter who our leaders are or what improvement programs we adopt.

We strive to practice what we preach—to operate our publishing company in line with the ideas in our books. At the core of our approach is stewardship, which we define as a deep sense of responsibility to administer the company for the benefit of all of our "stakeholder" groups: authors, customers, employees, investors, service providers, and the communities and environment around us.

We are grateful to the thousands of readers, authors, and other friends of the company who consider themselves to be part of the "BK Community." We hope that you, too, will join us in our mission.

A BK Business Book

This book is part of our BK Business series. BK Business titles pioneer new and progressive leadership and management practices in all types of public, private, and nonprofit organizations. They promote socially responsible approaches to business, innovative organizational change methods, and more humane and effective organizations.

Berrett–Koehler
Publishers

A community dedicated to creating
a world that works for all

Visit Our Website: www.bkconnection.com

Read book excerpts, see author videos and Internet movies, read our
authors' blogs, join discussion groups, download book apps, find out about
the BK Affiliate Network, browse subject-area libraries of books, get special
discounts, and more!

Subscribe to Our Free E-Newsletter, the *BK Communiqué*

Be the first to hear about new publications, special discount offers, exclu-
sive articles, news about bestsellers, and more! Get on the list for our free
e-newsletter by going to **www.bkconnection.com**.

Get Quantity Discounts

Berrett-Koehler books are available at quantity discounts for orders of ten or
more copies. Please call us toll-free at (800) 929-2929 or email us at **bkp
.orders@aidcvt.com**.

Join the BK Community

BKcommunity.com is a virtual meeting place where people from around
the world can engage with kindred spirits to create a world that works for
all. **BKcommunity.com** members may create their own profiles, blog, start
and participate in forums and discussion groups, post photos and videos,
answer surveys, announce and register for upcoming events, and chat with
others online in real time. Please join the conversation!